일빵빵 + 가장 많이 쓰는 영어표현

일빵빵
가장 많이 쓰는 영어표현

2018년 1월 20일 초판 1쇄 발행
2020년 8월 18일 초판 10쇄 발행

저 자 ｜ 서장혁
기 획 ｜ 일빵빵어학연구소
펴 낸 곳 ｜ 토마토출판사
주 소 ｜ 경기도 파주시 파주출판단지 회동길 216 2층
T E L ｜ 1544-5383
홈페이지 ｜ www.tomato4u.com
등 록 ｜ 2012. 1. 11.

일빵빵
가장많이쓰는
영어표현

토마토
출판사

더욱 새로워졌습니다

'일빵빵'어플 다운로드 받으시고
생생한 **원어민 선생님들**의 강의를 들어보세요.

※ 본 강의에 참여해 주신 Jason Nelson 선생님께 감사드립니다.

들어가며

영어 공부를 하다 보면
문장 안의 모든 단어를 알고 있는데도 무슨 뜻인지 아리송한 경우를 종종 만나게 됩니다. 이런 문장들은 따로 공부해 두지 않으면 절대 알 수 없죠.
이처럼 관용적으로 쓰이는 표현들은 다소 딱딱하고 지루한 영어를 좀 더 재미있고 유려하게 만드는 윤활제 역할을 합니다. 또한 같은 뜻을 전달하더라도 표현 선택의 폭을 늘려 주기도 합니다.

〈일빵빵 가장 많이 쓰는 영어표현〉은
다채로운 영어 구사를 돕기 위해 1,200여 개의 영어 표현을 추렸습니다. 수백만 개의 표현을 검토하면서 가장 중요하게 생각한 원칙은 '일상에서 쓰이는 표현일 것, 쓰이는 빈도수가 높을 것'입니다. 이를 위해 일빵빵이 직접 미국 현지에서 대학생 설문을 토대로 살아 숨 쉬는 표현들만 쏙쏙 골라서 수록했습니다.
문법과 어법만으로는 만들어 내기 힘든 생생한 1,200여 개의 표현들을 하나하나 공부하다 보면, 어느새 '미국에서 살다 오셨나 봐요'라는 말을 듣게 될 것입니다.

컨셉

"도대체 이걸 영어로 뭐라고 표현하지?"

이 물음에서부터 시작되었습니다.
우리가 평생 가장 많이 배우는 기초영어, 영어회화.
하지만 그런 기초적인 표현만으로는 외국인과 단 1분도 대화가 이어지지 않는다는 현실.
이제 그 해답을 이 책 한 권으로 시원하게 풀어 드릴 것입니다.

{   5년간 500여 개의 방송을 통해 노하우가 축적된
    빽빽한 컨텐츠 구성

{   일찍이 없었던, 200만 청취자와의 직접 피드백을 통해
    한국인 눈높이에 가장 알맞게 정리된 내용

{   집필진이 직접 미국으로 가서 현지 대학생들과 함께 연구한
    미국인들이 '가장 많이 쓰는' 1000여 개의 영어 표현 총정리

감정 표현

원어민들은 본인들이 직접 느끼고, 놀라고, 즐거워하거나 슬퍼할 때, 그 감정을 어떻게 한마디로 표현할까?

논리 표현

원어민들이 상대방에 대해 자신의 충고, 감사, 칭찬, 의견 등을 말할 때 적절한 표현은 무엇이 있을까?

부사 표현

미드나 영드를 보면 긴 문장으로 말하는 경우보다는 부사같이 짧은 단어만으로 의사 전달을 하는 경우가 있다. 그런 부사 표현에 대해 모두 정리해 보자.

위의 3가지 표현으로 나누어서 chapter별로 실제 영어 표현을 학습하도록 되어 있습니다.

일빵빵
가장 많이 쓰는
영어표현 ···

CONTENTS

2012년 6월 여름은 유난히 무더웠습니다.

너무나 멀어 보이는 길

아무도 가지 않은 길을 내딛었기에,

그래도 5년간 행복했고 뿌듯했습니다.

서로 보지는 못하고 잘 알지도 못했지만

끈끈히 유대된 팟캐스트 청취자들과

일빵빵의 역사를 함께 해 주신 독자분들을 위해

이 '가장 많이 쓰는' 시리즈를 바칩니다.

2017년 겨울 *서장혁*

가장 많이 쓰는

감정을 나타내는

영어 표현

느낌/기분

기쁨/즐거움/환희

슬픔/걱정/좌절

놀람/충격

불만/화남

CHAPTER 1
느낌/기분

001

빠져들어요.

I'm into it.

- into : ~ 안으로
= I'm really interested in that.
= I'm passionate about it.
  - passionate : 열정적인

002

웅장하다!

It's huge!

= It's large!

003

감동적이야!

It's so touching!

- touching : 마음에 닿는 / 감동적인
= It moves me.
  - move : 사물 / 마음을 움직이다

004

재미있네!

That's funny!

= That's amusing.
  - amusing : 재미있는

005

화끈해!

That's wild!

- wild : 야생의, 격렬한, 열광하는
= That's cool.

006

지루해.

It's boring.

- boring : 지루한
= That's not interesting.

007

시시해.

That was nothing.

= That's dull.
- dull : 따분한, 재미없는

008

졸려.

I'm sleepy.

= I'm drowsy.
- drowsy : 졸리는, 나른하게 만드는

009

죽인다!

So cool!

= It's amazing.
- amazing : 놀라운

010

느낌이 쎄-한데.

I have a bad feeling.

- feeling : (마음이나 감각을 통한) 느낌, 기분

느낌/기분

011

기분 나빠.
I feel bad.

= I'm in a bad mood.
- mood : 기분, 심기

012

기분 이상해.
I feel weird.

- weird : 이상한, 기이한
= I feel strange.

013

섬뜩해.
Creepy.

- creepy : 으스스한, 오싹한
= Scary.
= Frightening.
- frighten : ~을/를 겁먹게 하다

014

짜증나.
It's irritating.

- irritate : ~을/를 짜증나게 하다
= It's annoying.
- annoy : ~을/를 화나게 하다, 짜증나게 하다

015

위험할 것 같아.
It seems dangerous.

= It looks risky.
- risky : 위험한, 모험적인

016

오글거려.
Cheesy.

- 'Cheesy'는 '사람, 행위 등이 오글거리고 느끼하다'라는 표현.
cf) 'Oily'는 음식이 느끼할 때 사용하는 표현
ex) This pizza tastes too oily.

017

시원섭섭하다.
I feel bittersweet.

- bittersweet : 씁쓸하면서 달콤한,
괴로우면서도 즐거운

018

쩐다!
Awesome!

= Wonderful!

019

흥분돼.
I'm excited.

= I'm thrilled.
- thrill : ~을/를 열광시키다

020

만족해.
I am satisfied.

- satisfy : ~을/를 만족시키다
= I am happy with it.

CHAPTER 2
느낌/기분

021

부끄러워.
I'm embarrassed.

• embarrassed : (사람·행동이) 쑥스러운, 어색한

022

창피해. 수치스러워.
I'm ashamed.

• ashamed : (형용사) ~여서(해서) 부끄러운, 창피한

023

조금 쑥스럽다.
I'm a little shy.

= I'm a bit timid.
• timid : 소심한, 용기가 없는

024

관심 많아.
I'm really interested.

• be interested in something/someone
: ~에게 관심이 있다

025

관심 없어.
I'm not interested.

= I don't care about it.

026

당황스럽다.

I'm lost.

- lost : 동사 'lose'의 과거, 과거완료형
  ~을/를 잃다, 어떻게 할 줄 모르다
- = I'm at a loss.
  - be at a loss : 어쩔 줄 모르다

027

마음이 울적해.

I feel melancholy.

- melancholy : 우울한, 음침한
- = I feel down.

028

기분이 착잡해.

I have mixed feelings.

- mixed : (좋고 나쁜 것이) 뒤섞인

029

나 상처받았어.

I am hurt.

- hurt : 다치게 하다
- = I got offended.
  - offend : ~을/를 기분 상하게 하다

030

홀린 것 같아.

I feel possessed.

- possess : 소유하다, (자질·특징을) 지니다

느낌/기분

031

감흥이 없어.
Whatever.

- whatever : 그게 뭐든

032

또 오고 싶어.
I want to come again.

= I want to come back.

033

오늘은 무슨 일이 일어날 것 같아.
There's something in the air.

= Something might happen today.

034

기분이 오락가락해.
I feel like a mess.

= My feelings are all over the place.

035

어디서 이상한 냄새가 나.
Something smells weird.

= It stinks.
- stink : (고약한) 냄새가 나다, 악취가 풍기다

036

진짜 귀엽다!

It's so adorable!

- adorable : 사랑스러운, 귀여운
= It's super cute!

037

나 언짢아.

I'm upset.

- upset : 속상한, 마음이 상한
= I'm annoyed.
  - annoy : ~을/를 화나게 하다, 짜증나게 하다

038

너무 아까워!

Almost!

= That's too bad!

039

뭔가 할 기분이 아니야.

I'm not in the mood.

- be in the mood : 마음 내키다
- be in the mood for something
  : ~할 기분이다

040

혼자이고 싶어.

I wanna be alone.

- wanna : 'want to'의 줄임 표현
- alone : 혼자, 다른 사람 없이

041

해냈어!

I made it!

= I rocked it!
· rock : 마구 뒤흔들리다
= I nailed it!
· nail : (특히) 스포츠에서 ~을/를 이뤄 내다
= I aced it!
· ace : 완패시키다, 능가하다

042

들뜨는데!

I'm so hyper!

· hyper : 들뜬, 흥분한
= I can't wait.

043

네 덕분에 행복해.

You make me happy.

= You are my joy.
· joy : (큰) 기쁨, 환희

044

반가웠어.

It was a pleasure.

· pleasure : 기쁨, 즐거움
= It was nice seeing you.

045

기적 같은 일이야!

It's a miracle!

· miracle : 기적
= This can't be happening!

046

믿을 수가 없어.

I can't believe it.

= Is this a dream?

047

세상에, 그게 진짜였어?

Really?

= Was that true?
= Wow, that was real?

048

날아갈 것 같아.

I'm on cloud nine.

· **cloud nine** : 단테의 『신곡』에서 유래된, 천국
으로 가는 9번째 계단

= I'm in heaven!
= I'm walking on air.

049

내 직업에 만족해.

I like what I do.

= I enjoy my job.

050

이렇게 신날 수가!

How exciting!

· **exciting** : 신나는, 흥미진진한

051

이만큼 기쁜 건 처음이야!

I've never been this happy before!

= I've never felt so great!

052

환상적이야!

Terrific!

= Awesome!
= Fantastic!

053

짠! (놀라운 상황을 연출하면서)

Surprise!

• surprise : 놀라게 하다

054

짠! (물건을 내놓으면서)

Tada!

• Tada : 짜잔!
  = Voila!
  • voila : 자, 봐! (성공·만족을 나타냄/프랑스어)

055

맙소사!

OMG!

= Oh my Gosh!
= Holy Moly!
= Jeez!

056

만세!

Hurray!

= Yay!
= Yahoo!

057

너무 자랑스러워.

I am so proud of you.

• **be proud of** : ~을/를 자랑스러워하다
= You make me so proud.

058

굉장해!

Amazing!

= Cool!
= Excellent!

059

정말 행복한 하루였어.

It was a great day.

= Today was really amazing.

060

심장이 두근거려.

My heart is pumping.

• **pump** : (아래위·안팎으로 빠르게) 흔들리다,
　움직이다

= My heart is racing.
　• **race** : (두려움·흥분 등으로 뇌·심장 기능 등이)
　　바쁘게 돌아가다

기쁨/즐거움/환희

061

꿈만 같아.
It's like a dream.

= It's surreal.
· surreal : 비현실적인, 꿈 같은

062

살맛 나네!
Life is worth living!

· worth ~ ing : ~할 가치가 있는

063

완전 취향저격이야.
That's what I like.

= That's my favorite.

064

절로 웃음이 나.
It makes me smile.

= It brings me joy.

065

흐뭇해.
I'm delighted.

· delight : 기쁘게 하다
= I am satisfied.

CHAPTER 4
슬픔/걱정/좌절

066

울고 싶어.
I want to cry.

= I feel like crying.

067

너무 우울해.
I am so gloomy.

• **gloomy** : 어둑어둑한, 음울한
= I'm blue.
　• **blue** : 우울한

068

눈물이 멈추지 않아.
I cannot stop crying.

= I can't help but cry.
　• **can't help but** 동사원형/~ing
　　　　　　　　 : ~하지 않을 수 없다

069

그날 나 진짜 많이 울었어.
I cried a lot that day.

= I was in tears all day that day.

070

냅둬.
Leave me alone.

= I don't want to see anyone.

CHAPTER 4
슬픔/걱정/좌절

071

서럽다, 서러워.

I am really hurt.

= I am sad.
= I feel blue.

072

내가 아닌 것 같아.

I don't feel like myself.

• I don't feel like ~ : ~이/가 아닌 것 같은,
~할 생각이 없는

073

걱정 있어?

Any worries?

= What's wrong?
= Is everything OK?
= Is there any trouble with you?

074

일이 잘못되면 어떡하지?

What if something goes wrong?

= What if it doesn't work out?

075

난 안 될 거야.

This won't work out.

• work out : 효력이 있다, 일이 잘 진행되다
= I won't be able to make it.

076

오해가 있는 것 같아.

**There seems to be
a misunderstanding.**

· misunderstanding : 오해
= It looks like you missed something.
· miss : 놓치다

077

난 네가 걱정돼.

I am worried about you.

= You worry me.
= You make me nervous.
= You make me concerned.

078

머릿속이 복잡해.

I have so much to think about.

= I can't think straight.
= I'm overwhelmed.
· overwhelm : (격한 감정이) 휩싸다, 압도하다

079

이걸 어느 세월에 다 하지?

When will this be finished?

= How can I possibly do all this?
= When will this end?

080

자꾸 깜빡해서 큰일이야.

I am forgetting everything.

= I have been forgetful these days.

CHAPTER 4
슬픔/걱정/좌절

081

내 코가 석 자야.

I've got my own fish to fry.

- fry : (기름에) 굽다, 튀기다
  = I've got plenty to think about.
  - plenty : 풍부한 양
  = I am up to my ears in my own problems.
  - I am up to my ears in ~ : ~하느라 바쁘다

082

완전 쪽박 차게 생겼어.

I lost everything.

= I ended up with nothing.
- end : 끝나다

083

답이 없어.

There is no answer.

= I can't think of any solution.

084

다 그만두고 싶어.

I want to quit.

- quit : 관두다
  = I just want to leave everything behind.

085

다 나 때문이야.

It's all my fault.

- fault : 잘못
  = I am to blame for everything.
  - blame : 헐뜯다, 비난하다
  - be to blame : 비난받아 마땅하다

086

절망적이야.

It's so depressing.

• depressing : 우울한, 절망적인
= That's discouraging.
  • discourage : ~을/를 낙담시키다
= That's disheartening.
  • dishearten : ~을/를 낙심하게 하다

087

일이 잘 안 풀려.

It is not going well.

= It's not going anywhere.

088

내 힘으론 역부족이야.

It's too big of a job for me.

= That's too much for me.
= I can't handle this.
  • handle : 처리하다

089

패배자가 된 것 같아.

I feel like a loser.

• loser : 패배자, 왕따
= I'm a failure.
  • failure : 실패

090

난 멍청이야.

I feel so stupid.

= I'm so dumb.
  • dumb : 바보, 멍청이

31

CHAPTER 5
슬픔/걱정/좌절

091

세상이 내 마음 같지 않네.

Nothing works as I intended.

- intend : ~을/를 의도하다
  = It's not really going well like I expected.

092

힘들어.

I am so tired.

= I'm exhausted.
= I'm drained.
  - drain : (힘·돈 등을) 소모시키다

093

아무것도 못 하겠어.

I can't do anything.

- anything : 무엇, 아무것

094

오늘 기분 잡쳤어.

I am depressed today.

= I feel terrible today.
= I feel down today.

095

우울증 걸리겠어.

I am getting depressed.

- get depressed : 우울해지다

096

무기력해.

I feel weak.

- **weak** : 약한
  = I feel lazy.
  = I feel lethargic.
    - **lethargic** : 기면성의, 무기력한

097

혼란스러워.

I am so confused.

- **confuse** : 혼란스럽게 하다
  = I have so much on my mind.
  = I'm lost.

098

너무 답답해.

I am suffocating.

- **suffocate** : 질식사하다
  = I'm super annoyed.

099

또 그렇네.

Just my luck.

- **luck** : 운수

100

완전 파산이야.

I'm flat broke.

- **flat** : 평평한, 김빠진, 일언지하에
- **broke** : 파산한
  = I'm poor.
  = I'm penniless.
    - **penniless** : 무일푼의

CHAPTER 5
슬픔/걱정/좌절

101

나 망했어.

I screwed up.

• screw : 나사로 죄다, ~에 실수하다,
　　　　　망쳐 놓다 (up)

= I messed up.
= I failed.

102

말하자면 길어.

It's a long story.

= You don't need to know.

103

나 선택장애 같아.

I can't make a decision.

= I'm ambivalent.
　• ambivalent : (태도가) 양면적인
= I can't choose.
= I can't decide.

104

내 자신이 너무 부끄러워.

I am so ashamed of myself.

= I feel humiliated.
　• humiliate : 굴욕감을 주다
= I'm really embarrassed.
　• embarrass : ~을/를 당황하게 하다

105

계획이 물거품이 됐어.

The plan fell through.

• fall through : 완료되지 못하다

= It was all in vain.
　• in vain : 허사가 되어, 헛되이
= It came to nothing.

CHAPTER 6
놀람/충격

106

그게 정말이야?

Is that true?

= For real?
= Really?
= Are you serious?

107

대체 무슨 일이지?

What's happening?

= What's going on?
= What's the matter?
= What's the problem?

108

어쩌다 그랬니?

How did that happen?

= How come it possibly happened?

109

정말 난처해.

I am stuck.

• stuck : ~에 빠져 움직일 수 없는, 꼼짝 못 하는

110

말도 안 돼!

Unbelievable!

= That doesn't make sense.
  • make sense : 의미가 통하다, 이해가 되다

CHAPTER 6
놀람/충격

111

큰일 날 뻔했어.

That was close.

- close : 거의, 가까운
  = That was a close one.

112

믿을 수가 없어.

I can't believe it

- believe : ~을/를 믿다

113

설마!

You're kidding me!

- kid : 놀리다, 장난치다

114

세상에!

Oh, my goodness!

= Oh my Gosh!
= Oh Jeez!
= Holy Moly!
= Good Lord!

115

정말 끔찍해.

It's terrible.

= That's awful.
= That's horrible.

116

도저히 믿어지지 않아!

It can't be true!

= That can't be real.

117

생각지도 못했어.

I didn't even think about it.

= I couldn't think about it.
= I did not have that in mind.
= I wouldn't even think about it.

118

어떻게 그럴 수 있지?

How dare you?

• dare : 감히 ~하다
= How could you do that?
= How could you?

119

영문을 모르겠어.

No idea.

= I have no clue.
= I can't figure it out.
  • figure out : ~을/를 발견해 내다

120

조마조마해.

I am nervous.

• nervous : 떨린, 긴장한
= I'm anxious.
  • anxious : 불안해하는, 염려하는
= I feel uneasy.
  • uneasy : (마음이) 불안한, 우려되는

CHAPTER 6
놀람/충격

121

초조해서 미칠 것 같아.

It drives me crazy.

= It's driving me nuts.
- nuts : 미친, 제정신이 아닌

= It's driving me insane.
- insane : 정신 이상의, 미친

122

소름 돋아!

I got goosebumps!

- goosebumps : (추위·공포로 인한) 소름

= I got the creeps.
- creeps : 섬뜩해지는 느낌, 전율

123

그럴 리가 없어!

No way!

= That's impossible!

124

도대체 그게 무슨 경우야!

What in the world!

- in the world : 도대체

125

갑자기 생각이 안 나.

I just can't remember it now.

= I can't think of it.

126

그게 지금 무슨 소리야?

What are you talking about?

= What are you saying?
= What do you mean?
= What nonsense is that?

127

얼굴이 왜 이리 많이 상했니?

What happened to your face?

= Why do you look tired?

128

뜻밖인데?

This is unexpected.

· unexpected : 예상치 못한
= That's surprising.
= I never could have imagined.

129

그럴 리가.

That can't be.

· That can't be + (형용사) : ~일 리가 없다
(형용사 생략 가능)

ex) That can't be possible.
그게 가능할 리 없어.

130

어머나!

Oops!

= Gosh!
= O my!

131

네가 정말 싫어.

I hate you.

- **hate** : 싫다, 증오하다
  = I deeply dislike you.

132

마음에 안 들어.

I don't like it.

= It's not my style.

133

정말 별로다.

It is awful.

- **awful** : 끔찍한, 지독한
  = It's not great at all.
  = It's pretty bad.

134

완전 스트레스 받아.

I am getting too much stress.

= I'm super stressed out.
= I feel really anxious.

135

너무 불공평해.

It feels so unfair.

- **unfair** : 불공평한
  = It doesn't seem right to me.

136

너 이상해.

You are weird.

= You're strange.
= You're odd.

137

오늘 그럴 기분 아니야.

I don't feel like it today.

= I'm not in the mood today.

138

나한테 불만 있어?

**Do you have
some problem with me?**

= Do you have something against me?

139

너무 번거로워.

That's too much work.

= That's too much trouble.

140

시간이 없어.

We have no time

= There is no time to waste.
  • waste : 낭비하다

CHAPTER 7
불만/화남

141

사생활 좀 지켜 줘!

Give me my privacy!

- privacy : 사생활

142

욱하지 마.

Don't be short-tempered.

- short-tempered : 성급한, 성마른
  = Don't be so quick-tempered.
    - quick-tempered : 화를 잘 내는
  = Don't be so ill-tempered.
    - ill-tempered : 성질이 나쁜, 더러운

143

알다가도 모르겠네.

I will never get it.

- get it : 이해하다, 얻다
  = I will never understand.

144

봐주는 것도 하루 이틀이지.

I can't excuse you forever.

- excuse something/someone
  : (무례나 작은 실수 등을) 용서하다, 봐주다

145

귀찮아 죽겠어.

It's disturbing me so much.

- disturb : 귀찮게 하다, 방해하다
  = That's super annoying.
  = That's bothering me a lot.

146

내 물건 만지지 마.

Don't touch anything of mine.

= Don't touch my stuff.
= Keep your hands off my stuff.
 • keep one's hands off ~
  : ~로부터 손대지 못하게 하다

147

나 빼고 다 있어.

Everyone has it except me.

• except ~ : ~를 제외하고
= I'm the only one who does not have it.

148

굳이 지금 해야 돼?

Should I do it now?

= Must I do it now?

149

문자 씹혔어.

My text was ignored.

• ignore : 무시하다

150

어이가 없네.

I am speechless.

• speechless : 말 없는
= I have no words.
= I don't know what to say.

151

화내지 마.

Don't get angry.

= Don't get mad.

152

거짓말하지 마!

Don't lie!

= Tell the truth!

153

뒤통수 맞은 기분이야.

I feel betrayed.

• betray : (적에게 정보를) 넘겨주다,
배신(배반)하다

154

모든 게 엉망이야.

Everything is messed up.

• mess : 엉망진창으로 만들다
= It's all destroyed.
  • destroy : ~을/를 파괴시키다
= Everything is a disaster.
  • disaster : 재앙

155

그걸 왜 말한 거야?

Why are you telling me this?

• Why are you + 동사 ~ing
: 왜 ~을/를 하는 것이냐?

156

나보고 어쩌라고?

What do you want me to do?

= What am I supposed to do?
- be supposed to : ~하기로 되어 있다

157

너하고 할 말 없어.

I have nothing to say to you.

= I have no business with you.
- business : 사업, 상관, 관련

158

지금 나랑 장난해?

Are you serious?

= You've got to be kidding me right now?

159

너한테 난 뭐니?

What am I to you?

- What + be동사 + 주어 + to + 사람 '목적어'
  : ~에게 ~은/는 무엇이니?

ex) **What is she to him?**
그에게 그녀는 무엇이니?

160

어떻게 나한테 이럴 수 있어?

How could you do this to me?

= I can't believe you did this to me.

CHAPTER 8
불만/화남

161

귀여운 척하지 마.

Don't pretend to be cute.

• pretend to : ~인 체하다

162

내가 왜 화내는지 아니?

Do you know why I am angry?

= Don't you know why I am mad?

163

너한테 실망이야.

I am so disappointed.

= I'm really disappointed in you.

164

내가 어떻게 알아?

How do I know?

= How am I supposed to know?
= How could I possibly know?

165

넌 정말 구제 불능이야.

You are helpless.

= You're a hopeless case.
= You're a lost cause.
= You're incorrigible!
 • incorrigible : (나쁜 습관이) 고질적인, 구제 불능의

166

내 기대를 저버리지 마.
Don't let me down.

- **let me down** : 나의 기대를 저버리다
= Don't disappoint me.
= Don't fail me.

167

해도 해도 너무하네.
That's too much.

= You're going overboard.
- **go overboard** : ~에 대해 야단을 떨다
= You're going too far.

168

화가 머리끝까지 났어.
I am so pissed off.

- **piss off** : ~을/를 열 받게 하다
= I am so P.Oed.
- **P.Oed** : (은어적 표현) 화난, 짜증이 난
= I am really upset.

169

넌 쓰레기야!
You are a jerk!

- **jerk** : 얼간이
= You are an idiot.

170

내가 왜 참아야 돼?
Why do I have to be quiet?

= Why should I ignore this?
= Why should I say nothing?

171

가만있을 순 없어.

I can't stand it.

- stand : 참다
= I can't tolerate this.
  - tolerate : 참다, 견디다

172

이럴 때가 제일 싫어.

**I hate you the most
when you do this.**

- I + 동사원형 + 사람 '목적격' + the + 최상급
  : 나는 누군가가 ~하는 게 가장 ~하다
ex) I like you the most when you smile.
    나는 네가 웃을 때가 가장 좋아.

173

너답지 않아.

It doesn't look like you.

= You look like a completely other person.

174

나도 더는 안 참아.

I can't stand this anymore.

= I can't tolerate this anymore.

175

뚜껑 열리네.

You're pissing me off!

= You're making me upset!
= You irritate me.

176

내가 지금 진정하게 생겼어?

How can I calm down now?

· How can I + 동사원형 ~ ?
: 내가 어떻게 ~을/를 할 수 있겠어?

177

왜 항상 나야?

Why me?

= Why is it always me?

178

나한테 화났어?

Are you mad at me?

= Are you angry at me?

179

아니, 화 안 났는데?

No, I am not angry.

= No, I'm not mad at all.

180

삐졌어?

Are you mad?

= Are you annoyed?

181

화나지 않았어.
No, I am not mad.

= No, I am not upset.

182

기분 나쁠 뻔했어.
It almost hurt my feelings.

= I was about to get mad.

183

환장하겠네.
It drives me crazy.

= It drives me nuts.
= It drives me insane.

184

뒷골 땅긴다.
My blood pressure is rising.

· blood pressure : 혈압
· rise : (높은 위치·수준 등으로) 오르다, 올라가다

185

완전 낚였어.
It's all set up.

· set up : 함정
= It's all fake.
  · fake : 가짜의, 모조품
= I got tricked.
  · trick : 속임수, 장난

186

한 번만 더 그래 봐.

If you do it one more time…

= Don't you ever do this again!

187

그래서 요점이 뭐야?

So what is your point?

· point : 요점, 핵심

= So what are you trying to say?

188

지금 나랑 해보자는 거야?

You got a problem?

· got a problem : 문제가 생기다

189

무슨 이런 경우가 다 있어?

What's all about this?

cf) What's all this about?
이게 다 뭐니?

190

너 방금 뭐 한 거야?

What did you just do?

= What have you just done?

가장 많이 쓰는
논리를 나타내는
영어 표현

CHAPTER 10
충고/조언/의무

191

섣불리 판단하지 마.

Don't judge a book by its cover.

- cover : 표지
= Don't judge people based on their appearance.
- appearance : 외모

192

입장 바꿔 생각해 봐.

Put yourself in my shoes.

- put oneself in one's shoes/place
: ~의 입장이 되어 생각하다

193

한 번 더 생각하고 말해.

Think before you speak.

= Speak carefully.
조심스레 얘기해, 생각하고 말해.

194

떼쓰면 안 돼.

Stop begging.

- beg : 간청하다, 애원하다

195

좋을 때도 있고 나쁠 때도 있는 거야.

Life is bittersweet.

- bittersweet : 씁쓸하면서 달콤한, 괴로우면서도 즐거운

196

날 물로 보지 마.
I'm stronger than you think.

= I am not as weak as you imagine.

197

빙빙 돌리지 마.
Get to the point.

= Stop beating around the bush.
그만 돌려서 이야기해.
• beat : ~을/를 치다, 때리다
• bush : 덤불

198

그래 봤자 소용없어.
It won't work.

= There is no point to this.

199

전화를 하지 마.
Don't call.

• call : (호칭을) 부르다, 전화하다

200

지금 당장 가!
Leave right now!

= Go away now!

CHAPTER 10
충고/조언/의무

201

네가 항상 옳진 않아.

You are not always right.

= You're wrong sometimes.

202

시간이 없어, 서둘러!

Come on, we don't have time!

= Hurry, there is no time to waste!

203

현실적으로 생각해.

Think realistically.

• **realistically** : 현실적으로
= Stop dreaming.

204

담배를 끊는 게 좋아.

You better quit smoking.

= You really should stop smoking.

205

평생 부모에게 의지하면 안 돼!

Stop clinging to your parents!

• **cling to** : ~에게 달라붙다, 의지하다
= Don't depend on your parents too much!
　• **depend on** : ~에게 의존하다

206

오늘 안에 다 해야 돼.

Finish it up by today.

= Get it done by today.

207

좀 더 모질게 해.

You should be tougher.

• **tough** : 힘든, 어려운
= Act stronger.

208

다른 사람 좀 배려하면서 살아!

Be nice to others!

= Be kind to those around you!

209

일찍 자고 일찍 일어나.

Go to bed early, get up early.

• **go to bed** : 잠자리에 들다
• **get up** : 일어나다, 기상하다

210

돈 좀 아껴.

Save some money.

• **save** : 아끼다, 절약하다
= Don't spend too much.

CHAPTER 11
충고/조언/의무

211

운전 좀 똑바로 해.

Hold on to the wheel.

- hold on to ~ : ~을 계속 잡고 있다, 계속 지키다
- wheel : 운전대

212

쓰레기 분리 좀 제대로 해.

Why don't you recycle?

- recycle : 재활용하다, 재생하다

213

너 연습 좀 더 해야겠다.

You should practice
more and more.

- practice : 연습하다
  = You really should get more practice.

214

말로만 하지 말고 보여 줘.

Stop talking about it and show me.

= Don't talk, act.

215

형이 모범을 보여야지.

An older brother should
set an example.

- set an example : 모범을 보이다,
  본보기가 되다

216

그런 식으로 말하면 안 돼.

Don't put it like that.

= Don't say it that way.

217

그만 싸워.

Stop arguing.

• argue : 논쟁하다, 다투다
= Stop fighting.

218

차근차근 해 나가야지.

Go step by step.

• step by step : 천천히, 단계적으로
= Go one step at a time.

219

지킬 건 지켜야지.

Keep the rules!

• rules : 룰, 규칙
= Follow the rules!

220

질문하는 걸 두려워하지 마!

Don't be afraid of asking questions!

= Feel free to ask questions.
• feel free to ~ : 마음대로 ~하세요

충고/조언/의무

221

자기 안전은 자기가 챙겨야지.
Take care of yourself.

· take care of oneself
: ~을/를 잘 챙기다, 관리하다

222

위험해질 거야.
You will put yourself in danger.

= You will get in trouble.

223

자세 똑바로 해.
Sit up straight.

= Watch your posture.
· posture : (사람이 앉거나 서 있는) 자세

224

자연스럽게 행동해.
Be natural.

= Be yourself.
= Just be who you are.

225

너무 힘이 들어갔어.
You are too tense.

· tense : 사람이 긴장한, 신경이 날카로운

226

너 지금 잘못하고 있어.

You're making a mistake.

= You're doing it wrong!

227

너 그러다 버릇된다.

Don't get used to it.

• get used to ~ : ~에 익숙해지다
= You will get accustomed to it.

228

그러다 허리 굽는다.

You will hurt your back.

• hurt one's + 명사 : 누군가의 ~을/를 다치게
하다, 상하게 하다

229

억지로 먹지 마.

You do not need to eat it all.

= You don't have to eat everything.

230

말실수 하지 마.

Don't make any mistakes.

= Don't do anything wrong.

CHAPTER 12
충고/조언/의무

231

가까운 사이일수록 조심해야 돼.

Be good to your friends.

- be good to ~ : ~에게 잘하다

232

나쁜 소식은 빨리 듣는 게 나아.

**It's better to get the hard part
over with first.**

= It's best to begin with what's most
difficult.

233

내 충고를 듣지 그랬어?

Why didn't you take my advice?

- advice : 충고
  = Why didn't you follow my suggestion?
  - follow : 따르다
  - suggestion : 제안

234

언젠가 탄로 날 거야.

It will come out someday.

- come out : 드러나다
  = It will be revealed someday.
  - reveal : (비밀 등을) 드러내다, 밝히다

235

네 말에 책임져야 돼.

**You are responsible for
what you say.**

- responsible : 책임 있는
  = You should take responsibility for
  your words.

236

그게 끝일 수 있어.

That could be it.

= That could be the end of everything.

237

꿈도 꾸지 마!

You wish!

= In your dreams!
= Don't even think about it!

238

너 나한테 신세 졌어.

You owe me.

• owe : 빚지다, 신세 지다
= You should thank me.

239

정신 차려.

Get a grip.

• grip : 꽉 잡다 / 움켜쥠
= Put yourself together.
= Wake up!

240

집중해.

Concentrate.

= Focus.

충고/조언/의무

241

정도껏 해라.

Know your limits.

- limits : 한계
= Don't do too much.

242

조언이 필요해?

Do you need advice?

= Do you need any tips?
- tips : 조언

243

진정해. 침착해.

Calm down.

= Hold on to your horses.
- horse : 말, 경마

244

가서 좀 쉬어.

Take a rest.

= Take a break.

245

규칙적인 생활을 해.

**You should get on
a regular schedule.**

- regular : 규칙적인
= You should have a routine.
- routine : 규칙

246

가지면 가질수록 더 원하게 되어 있어.

Greed leads to greed.

- greed : 탐욕
- lead to ~ : ~로 이끌다
  = The more you get, the more you want.

247

이성적으로 생각해.

Think rationally.

- rationally : 이성적으로
  = Be rational about it.

248

익숙해지는 수밖에.

You'd better get used to it.

- get used to ~ : ~에 익숙해지다
  = You'd better get familiar with it.
  - get familiar with ~ : ~에 친근하다

249

말하지 않는 게 좋겠어.

Keep this a secret.

= Keep your mouth shut.
  - shut : 닫다

250

긴장 풀어. / 쉬엄쉬엄해.

Take it easy.

= Chill out.
  - chill : 냉기, 한기
= Relax.
= Calm down.

CHAPTER 13
충고/조언/의무

251

조급해하지 마.

Don't rush.

• **rush** : (너무 급히) 서두르다
= Take your time.

252

그 말은 위로가 안 돼.

It won't be of any help.

= That's not helpful.

253

이게 요즘 유행이야.

It's the hottest thing.

= It's super popular.

254

내 말 좀 들어.

Please listen to me.

• **listen to** + 명사 : ~을/를 듣다, 귀를 기울이다

255

아플 땐 죽을 먹어.

Have some soup if you are sick.

= Eat well, sleep well when you are ill.

256

인생 한 방이야.

You only live once. (YOLO)

= Life is unexpected.

257

조심해서 나쁠 것 없어.

Better to be safe than sorry.

• **better to be** + 형용사 : ~하는 것이 낫다

258

목숨은 소중한 거야.

Life is precious.

• precious : 값진
= Life is a gift.
= Don't take your life for granted.
　• take something/someone for granted
　　　: ~을/를 당연하게 여기다

259

그건 다 환상이야.

That only happens in the movies.

= That never happens in real life.

260

검색하면 다 나와.

You can search for anything.

• search for ~ : ~을/를 찾다

CHAPTER 13
충고/조언/의무

261

사는 게 다 그렇지.

That's life.

= That's how it is.

262

스펙을 쌓아 둬야 돼.

You need to be well-rounded.

· **well-rounded** : 다재다능한, 전인격을 갖춘

263

아직은 때가 아니야.

It is not the right time.

= It's not the best time.
= It's not the right moment.

264

내일로 미뤄.

Do it tomorrow.

= Put it off to tomorrow.
= Postpone it to tomorrow.

265

참고로 적어 놔.

Write it down for reference.

· **write down** : 받아 적다
· **reference** : 참고, 참조
= Take some notes for later.

266

나이는 중요하지 않아.

Age does not matter.

= Age is only a number.

267

인생은 타이밍이야.

Life is about timing.

= It's all about timing.

268

다 그렇게 말해.

Everyone says that.

= Everyone says exactly the same thing.

269

고민할 가치도 없어.

**It is a waste of time
to think about it.**

= There's no reason to waste time on this.
= It's not worth it.

270

기억에서 지워.

Forget it.

= Stop thinking about it.

271

허튼소리 하지 마.

Don't be foolish.

- foolish : 바보 같은
  = Don't be silly.
    - silly : 어리석은
  = Don't be stupid.

272

네가 책임져.

You take responsibility.

= You should be responsible for this issue.
  - responsibility : (명사) 책임(감)
  - responsible : (형용사) ~에 대해 책임이 있는

273

말꼬리 잡지 마.

Don't play around with me.

- play around with : ~을/를 데리고 놀다
  = Don't fool around with me.
    - fool around with ~ : ~와 장난치다

274

제발 좀 그만해.

Please stop.

= Would you please cut it out!

275

그건 핑계야.

That's an excuse.

- excuse : 변명, 핑계
  = Don't make an excuse.

276

창피한 줄 알아!

Shame on you!

· shame : (자기가 한 짓에 대해 갖는) 수치심

= You should be ashamed of yourself!

277

너 많이 컸다?

You have changed.

= You're not the same.

278

너 진짜 노답이다.

You are helpless.

· helpless : 무력한, 속수무책인

= You are out of control.

279

너 정말 비열하다.

You are so mean.

· mean : 비열한

= You're so terrible.

= You're so horrible.

= You are so nasty.

280

철 좀 들어!

Grow up!

= Act your age!

= Don't be so childish!

CHAPTER 14
질책/비난

281

그걸 왜 나한테 묻니?

Why do you even ask me?

= How could I possibly answer this?

282

그러게 누가 속으래?

You shouldn't have trusted it.

- **trust** : 믿다
= You shouldn't have believed that.
= Don't believe everything (you see/hear…)

283

내가 말할 때 들었어야지.

You should have listened to me.

= You should have followed my suggestions.

284

성질 좀 죽여.

Don't be hot-tempered.

= Don't be short-tempered.

285

모르는 척하지 마.

Don't pretend you don't know.

- **pretend** : ~인 척하다 (~인 것처럼 굴다)

286

설마 기억 못하는 건 아니지?

You didn't forget this, did you?

= Don't tell me you don't remember.

287

정신을 어디다 두고 다녀?

**You'd lose your head
if it weren't bolted on.**

• **bolt** : 빗장, 볼트
　　　　빗장을 지르다, 볼트로 접합하다

= Are you crazy?
= Are you insane?

288

눈은 장식이니?

Don't you have eyes?

= Can't you see?
= Are you blind?

289

너답지 않게 왜 이래?

What's wrong with you?

= What's your problem?

290

나다운 게 뭔데?

What's wrong with me?

= Is there something wrong with me?

CHAPTER 15
질책/비난

291

내 얘기 제대로 들었어?

Did you hear what I said?

= Did you catch what I said?

292

어떤 부분이 이해가 안 돼요?

**Which part
don't you understand?**

= What's the part you don't get?

293

제발 닥쳐.

Shut your mouth.

= Shut up!
= Shut it.
= Be quiet.

294

넌 그게 문제야.

That's your problem.

= That's your issue.

295

또 잊어버렸어?

You forgot it again?

• forget something : 무엇을 잊어버리다
cf) lose something : 무엇을 잃어버리다

296

넌 그거 고쳐야 돼.

You have to fix it.

- have to : ~을/를 해야만 하다
- fix : 고치다

297

사회생활 안 해 본 티가 난다.

You are new to this, huh?

= You've never been in this kind of thing before, right?

298

우리 때는 이런 거 상상도 못했어.

I couldn't even imagine.

- imagine : 상상하다

= It was hard to imagine back in our times.

299

말투 좀 고쳐.

Watch your tone.

- tone : 톤, 음색

= Watch your mouth.
= Watch your tongue.

300

어디서 꼬박꼬박 말대답이야?

Stop arguing with me.

- argue : 논쟁하다, 다투다

= Stop talking back to me.

CHAPTER 15
질책/비난

301

이럴 거면 때려치워.

Stop if you're not going to do it right.

= Just leave it if you can't do it properly.

302

사람들이 널 싫어해.

People hate you.

= No one likes you.

303

너 정말 개념 없어.

You lack common sense.

- lack : 부족하다
- common sense : 상식, 양식

304

봐주니까 우습니?

You think I am playing with you?

= You think I am fooling with you?

305

있을 때 잘해.

Take care of me while I'm still with you.

- take care of ~ : ~을/를 잘 돌보다
- while + 주어 + 동사 : ~이/가 ~하는 동안

306

분위기 파악 좀 해!

Understand your surroundings!

· surroundings : 주변 환경
= Don't break the mood!

307

같은 말 반복하게 하지 마.

Don't make me repeat myself.

· repeat : 반복하다
= Don't make me say it again.

308

넌 너무 못됐어.

You are messed up.

= You are mean.
= You're really bad!

309

이제 네 일에 신경 끌래.

I won't get involved in your life.

· involve : 관계 맺다, 연관 짓다
= I'll stay out of your life.

310

너에게서 벗어나고 싶어.

I want to get away from you.

= I want to run away from you.
= I don't want to hear from you anymore.

CHAPTER 16
질책/비난

311

악몽 같아.

It was a nightmare.

= It was a bad dream.

312

정말 한심해.

You are pathetic.

• pathetic : 한심한

= You are miserable.

• miserable : 비참한

313

네 꼴 좀 봐.

Look at you.

• look at ~ : ~을/를 보다
• look at you : 어떤 사람의 행동에 비꼬는 듯
이 말함

314

그렇게 살지 마.

You shouldn't live like that.

= You should really change your ways.

315

네가 어린애니?

You are so childish!

= You are really immature.

• immature : 미성숙한

316

네가 지금 무슨 일을 했는지 알아?

Do you know what you just did?

= Are you aware of what you did just now?
· be aware of : 알아차리다

317

넌 너무 파렴치해!

You are shameless.

· shameless : 창피한 줄 모르는, 파렴치한

318

허세 부리지 마.

Don't brag.

· brag : (심하게) 자랑하다
= Stop showing off.
· show off : 과시하다, 자랑하다

319

입 함부로 놀리지 마.

Watch your mouth.

= Watch your tongue.
= Watch your language.
= Watch your words.

320

잘난 척하지 마.

Stop showing off.

· show off : ~을/를 자랑하다
= Don't brag so much.
· brag : (심하게) 자랑하다
= Don't boast about it.
· boast : 뽐내다, 자랑하다

CHAPTER 16
질책/비난

321

참 우유부단하다.

You are so indecisive.

- indecisive : 우유부단한, 결단을 못 내리는
  = You are so hesitant.
  - hesitant : 주저하는, 망설이는

322

컴퓨터 다운됐잖아.

The computer crashed.

- crash : (차량이나 운전자가) 충돌하다, 들이받다,
  (컴퓨터가) 갑자기 서 버리다, 고장 나다

323

이제 어쩔 거야?

What are you going to do now?

= What's your plan?
= So what now?

324

앓는 소리 하지 마.

Stop whining.

- whine : 징징거리다, 칭얼거리다
  = Stop complaining.

325

양심이 있어야지.

You don't have any conscience.

- conscience : 양심
  = You have no scruples.
  - scruples : (주로 복수로 쓰여) 양심, (양심의) 가책

326

너 꼰대 같아.

**You are acting like
a grumpy old man.**

- act like : ~처럼 행동하다
- grumpy : 성미 까다로운, 심술궂은

327

책임 전가하지 마.

**Don't try to avoid
your responsibility.**

- avoid : 피하다
  = Don't run away from responsibilities.

328

네가 무능한 탓이야.

Blame yourself.

- blame : 탓하다
  = It's the player, not the basketball.

329

조심하라고 몇 번을 말하니?

**How many times
should I warn you?**

= How many times should I tell you?

330

자업자득이다.

You deserve it.

- deserve : ~을/를 받을 만하다,
  ~을/를 당해야 마땅하다

CHAPTER 17
질책/비난

331

너나 나나 똑같아.
We are in the same boat.

= We're in this together.
= We're in the same situation.

332

멍 때리지 마!
Wake up!

= Stop spacing out!
· space : 공간

333

퍽이나 그렇겠다.
Yeah, right~

= Sure···

334

나잇값 좀 해.
Act like an adult.

= Act your age.
= Don't be so childish.
= Don't be so immature.

335

넌 너무 조심성이 없어.
You're not being cautious.

· cautious : 조심스러운
= You're not careful enough.

336

그러기에 조심했어야지.

You should have been careful.

= You had to be more cautious.

337

언제까지 일일이 챙겨 줘야 돼?

**How long
should I take care of you?**

= How long will I have to watch over you?
  • watch over : ~을/를 보살피다, 보호하다

338

또 삐쳤어?

Are you mad again?

= Are you angry again?
= Are you upset again?

339

얼씨구?

Hello?

= Are you crazy?

340

아무짝에도 쓸모없는 놈.

You are useless.

= You are good for nothing.

CHAPTER 17
질책/비난

341

너 때문에 못살겠다.

I can't stand you.

= I can't tolerate you.

342

갑질하지 마.

Stop being bossy.

• **bossy** : 우두머리 행세를 하는
= Stop trying to control everything.

343

할 일이 없어?

Don't you have anything to do?

= Don't you have a life?

344

오타쿠 같아.

You are a geek.

• **geek** : 괴짜
= You are a total nerd.
  • **nerd** : 샌님, 컴퓨터만 아는 괴짜
= You're such a freak.
  • **freak** : ~에 광적으로 관심이 많은 사람

345

패션 테러리스트야.

You have no sense of fashion.

= Your fashion is out of style.
  • **out of style** : 유행이 지난

346

변태 같아.
You are a pervert.

• pervert : (시스템·절차 등을) 왜곡하다,
(사람을) 비뚤어지게 하다, 변태

347

말 똑바로 해.
Speak clearly.

• clearly : 또렷하게, 분명히, 알기 쉽게

348

돼지우리가 따로 없네!
It's a pigsty!

• pigsty : 돼지우리
= It's such a mess!

349

그걸 보고만 있었어?
Did you just watch it?

= Were you just looking on it?

350

찌질이 같아.
You are a loser.

= You have no future.

CHAPTER 18
질책/비난

351

하루 종일 삽질했어.

We worked for nothing today.

= Everything we did today was in vain.
• in vain : 허사가 되어, 헛되이

352

완전 여우 짓 하잖아.

She is deceitful.

• deceitful : 기만적인, 부정직한
= Cunning like a fox.
• cunning : 교활한, 간사한

353

버릇없어.

He's spoiled.

• spoil : ~이 상하다/예의가 없다

354

글러 먹었어.

No class.

• class : 우아함, 탁월함, 품위

355

누가 그렇게 하래?

Whose idea is this?

= Who thought about this?

356

그런 말은 어디서 배운 거야?

Where did you learn that word?

= How do you know that word?

357

왜 이렇게 복잡해?

Why is it so complicated?

· **complicated** : 복잡한
= Why does it have to be so hard?
= Why is it so difficult?

358

넌 눈치가 없어.

You have no tact.

· **tact** : 요령, 눈치
= You have no sense.

359

취향 존중해 줄래?

Can you respect my preference?

· **preference** : 기호, 취향
= Can you please take into
  consideration what I like?

360

진작 말했어야지!

You should have said so!

= You should have mentioned that before!

361

그렇게 말해도 소용없어.

There's no need to talk like that.

= There's no point in saying that.

362

그 말을 믿니?

Do you believe that?

= Do you trust that?

363

치사해.

You are awful.

= You are playing dirty.

364

이게 말이야 방귀야?

What you say doesn't make sense.

= That's pure nonsense!
= That's ridiculous.
= That's completely absurd!
  • absurd : 우스꽝스러운, 터무니없는

365

말로는 안 되겠다.

Words aren't enough.

= That's it.

366

말 같지도 않은 소릴 하네.

You're not making any sense.

= You make no sense.

367

어디서 그런 못된 말을 배웠어?

**Where did you learn
such words?**

= Who taught you to speak that way?

368

말로는 누가 못해?

Talk is cheap.

= That's easier said than done.

369

거짓말이지?

You are lying.

= You're not telling the truth, are you?

370

차라리 말을 마.

Just be quiet.

= Just shut it.
= Shush.
= Shut your mouth.

CHAPTER 19
감사

371

여러모로 고마워.

Thank you for everything.

= I am grateful for what you've done.
  • grateful : 고마워하는, 감사하는
= I appreciate everything you've done.
  • appreciate : 고마워하다, 환영하다

372

이러지 않아도 되는데!

You don't have to do this!

• do not have to + 동사원형 : ~하지 않아도 되다

373

네 덕분에 살았어.

You saved my life.

• save : (죽음·손상·손실 등에서) 구하다

374

많은 도움이 됐어.

It was helpful.

= It really helped me.

375

생각도 못 했어!

I couldn't even think about it!

• not even : ~조차 않다
• think about : ~에 대해 생각하다, 고려하다

376

생명의 은인이야!

He is a life saver!

= He saved my life.

377

이 은혜를 어떻게 갚아야 할지…

How can I pay this back?

= How can I thank you for everything?

378

여기까지 와 줘서 고마워.

Thank you for coming here.

= Thanks for your presence.
· presence : 존재(함), 참석

379

항상 챙겨 줘서 고마워.

Thank you for taking care of me,
always.

= Thanks for always being there for me.

380

고생해 줘서 고마워.

Thanks for your effort.

= Thank you for your hard work.

CHAPTER 19
감사

381

영광이야. / 과찬이야.

I'm so flattered.

- **flatter** : 아첨하다, 알랑거리다
  = I thank you for the compliment.
    - **compliment** : 찬사, 칭찬

382

정말 감사드립니다.

I really appreciate it.

= I can't thank you enough.
= I am sincerely grateful.
  - **sincerely** : 진심으로

383

응원 고마워.

Thank you for the support.

= Thank you for believing in me.

384

초대해 줘서 고마워.

Thank you for inviting me.

= Thanks for the invitation.

385

불러 줘서 고마워.

Thank you for having me.

= Thank you for welcoming me here today.

386

마음만으로도 고마워.

It's the thought that counts.

• count : (수량을) 헤아리다, 여기다, 중요하다

387

귀띔해 줘서 고마워!

Thanks for the heads-up!

• heads-up : 미리 알려 주는 정보 또는 주의
= I appreciate the advice.

388

알려 줘서 고마워.

Thank you for letting me know.

= Thanks for telling me.

389

네가 있어서 다행이야.

I am so glad to be with you.

= Your presence makes me so happy.

390

네 고생을 잊지 않을게.

I will never forget what you did.

= I will always remember what you did.
= I will always keep in mind what you did.

감사

391

위로해 줘서 고마워.

Thank you for comforting me.

• comfort : 편안함, 위로, 위안
= Thanks for making me feel better.
= Thanks for cheering me up.

392

고마워, 잘 쓸게.

Thank you,
I will put it to good use.

= Thank you, it'll be really useful.

393

천만에.

You bet.

• bet : 내기하다, ~이 틀림없다
= No worries.
= No problem.

394

천만에.

You're welcome.

= My pleasure.

395

천만에.

No problem.

= It was nothing.

396

잘했어.

Well done.

= Good job.
= Great job.
= Bravo.
= You rock.
= Wonderful.
= Splendid.

397

정말 대단한데?

Amazing.

= Awesome.
= Astonishing.
= Incredible.
= Fantastic.

398

그래, 그거야.

Right.

= That's it.
= That's exactly it.
= That's what I mean.

399

대견해./기특해.

I am proud of you.

• **be proud of** + 명사 : ~을/를 자랑스러워하다,
대견해하다

ex) **I'm proud of your work.**
나는 너의 작품이 자랑스러워.

400

너를 다시 봤어.

Better than expected.

= I didn't expect that much.
= That's over my expectations.

CHAPTER 20
칭찬/축하

401

견줄 게 없어.
You are the best.

= There's nothing in the world better than you.

402

네가 잘 돼서 나도 기뻐.
I am happy for you.

= Congratulations.

403

네가 부럽다.
I envy you.

= I am so jealous of you.

404

해낼 줄 알았어!
I knew you could do it!

= I knew you'd make it!

405

수고 많았어.
Good effort.

• **effort** : 수고, 애 / 노력, 공

406

고생했어.

Good job.

= Well done.

407

세상에서 제일 예뻐.

You are the greatest.

· You are the + 최상급 : 네가 제일 ~하다
ex) You are the smartest.
　　네가 제일 똑똑해.

408

너 혹시 천재 아니야?

Are you a genius?

= You're so smart.

409

앞으로 더 잘할 거야.

You will be better.

You'll get better.

= You'll do better from now on.

410

넌 눈이 참 예뻐.

You've got pretty eyes.

= Your eyes are beautiful.

칭찬/축하

411

최고야! 훌륭해!

Excellent!

= Splendid!
= Wonderful!
= Fantastic!

412

넌 일 처리가 빨라.

You work so fast.

= You're so quick.

413

너는 못하는 게 없구나!

You are capable of everything!

• be capable of : ~할 수 있다

= You really are a Jack of all trades!
• Jack of all trades : 무엇이나 다 하는 사람,
만물박사

414

노력하는 모습 보기 좋아.

**You look great
when you work hard.**

• You look + 형용사 : ~해 보이다
ex) You look beautiful today.
너 오늘 진짜 예뻐 보여.

415

웃는 모습이 예뻐.

You've got a pretty smile.

= I love it when you smile.
= You are pretty when you smile.

416

요즘 잘 되는 것 같아.

Things are going well these days.

= Everything is going great these days.

417

네 노력이 보상받을 줄 알았어.

I knew you would be rewarded.

• reward : 보상하다
= I knew your efforts would pay off.
　• pay off : 성공하다

418

너 같은 남자도 없어.

I can't find a man like you.

= There is no man like you.

419

그 애를 보기만 해도 기분이 좋아져.

He's eye-candy.

• eye-candy : 눈으로 보기에 좋은 사람, 사물
= I feel great when he's around.

420

어쩜 그렇게 귀엽니?

You're so cute!

= You're so adorable.
　• adorable : 사랑스러운

CHAPTER 21
칭찬/축하

421

나도 너처럼 되고 싶어.
I want to be like you.

= I wish I could be like you.

422

넌 정말 말을 잘해!
You're a great speaker!

= You speak really well!

423

넌 개그맨 같아.
You are like a comedian.

= You're hilarious.
- hilarious : 아주 우스운, 재미있는

424

네가 없었다면 난 끔찍했을 거야.
I would be miserable without you.

- miserable : 끔찍한
= I don't know what i'd do without you.

425

내 친구한테 너를 칭찬했어.
I complimented you in front of my friend.

- compliment : 칭찬하다
= I said good things about you to my friend.

426

우리 부모님도 널 칭찬하더라.

My parents also said good things about you.

= My parents also praised you.

427

은근히 좋아.

I secretly like you.

• **secretly** : 비밀히, 내밀히
= I kind of like you.

428

네가 최고야.

You rock!

= You're amazing!
= You're awesome!
= You're the best!

429

최고야!

Fantastic!

= Wonderful.
= Admirable.
= Outstanding.
= Exceptional.
= Magnificent.

430

잘 해냈어!

Way to go!

= Good job!
= Well done!
= Amazing work!
= You nailed it!
  • **nail** : (특히 스포츠에서) ~을 이루어 내다

431

너 볼매다.
You look better everyday.

= You are really attractive.

432

너 정말 깔끔하구나.
You are neat.

• **neat** : 단정한, 깔끔한
= You are well-arranged.
  • **arranged** : 정리된

433

어른 같아.
You seem mature.

• **mature** : 성숙한
= You act like an adult.

434

넌 정말 젠틀해.
You are so gentle.

= You are truly kind.
= You are very considerate.

435

너는 참 좋은 여자야.
You are a nice woman.

= You are such a great woman.
= You are truly an amazing woman.

436

참 착한 아이구나.

You are so kind.

= You are such a good person.

437

넌 참 똑똑해.

You are so smart.

= You're so intelligent.
= You are such a brilliant person.
   • brilliant : 빛나는, 영특한

438

입학 축하해!

Congrats on getting in!

• get in : 들어오다, 입학하다
= Congratulations on your acceptance.
= Congrats on being accepted.

439

졸업 축하해.

Congrats on your graduation.

= Kudos to you for getting your degree!
   • kudos : 영광, 영예, 칭찬

440

승진 축하해.

Congrats on your promotion.

• promotion : 승진
= Congratulations on getting promoted.

441

그 애는 참 야무져.

He is well-rounded.

• **well-rounded** : 다재다능한, 전인격성의
= He's intelligent.
= He's brilliant.

442

그 애는 참 영악해.

He is cunning.

• **cunning** : 교활한
= He is as sly as a fox.
  • **sly** : (행동 따위가) 교활한, 음흉한

443

그 애는 참 털털해.

He is easy-going.

• **easy-going** : (성격이) 느긋한, 태평스러운

444

저 사람 진상이다.

She is a jerk.

= She's an idiot.

445

저 사람 좀 이상해.

He is weird.

= He is a weirdo.
= He's strange.
= He's a freak.

446

그 사람 특이해.

He is a little unusual.

· unusual : 독특한, 특이한
  = He is unique.
  = He is one of a kind.

447

걔는 덜렁대.

She is clumsy.

· clumsy : 덜렁대는
  = She's all thumbs.
  · all thumbs : 몹시 서툴고 어색한 것

448

쟨 정말 공붓벌레/일벌레야.

He is a nerd/workaholic.

· nerd : (공부·취미 따위만 파고드는) 따분한 사람, 샌님
· workaholic : 일 중독자, 일벌레

449

쟤는 참 곰 같아.

He is dull.

  = He's dumb.
  = He's not too sharp.

450

그분은 참 인자해.

He is very generous.

· generous : 관대한, 인자한
  = He's so big-hearted.

CHAPTER 22
평가/판단

451

요즘 애들 이상해.

Kids are weird these days.

= Young people are strange these days.

452

정말 치열하다.

Highly competitive.

• **competitive** : 경쟁을 하는
= Cut-throat.
  • **cut-throat** : 경쟁이 치열한, 먹느냐 먹히냐의

453

역대급이다.

Legendary.

= Famous.
= Well-known.
= Celebrated.

454

'걔네들만의 리그'야. (비유적 표현)

It's a different world.

= They're living in a different world.

455

이런 광경은 처음이야.

I've never seen something like this.

= It's the first time I see something like this.

456

돈이 아깝지 않아.

It's worth to paying for it.

= It's worth paying for.

457

눈물 없인 들을 수 없어.

I can't help crying.

= I can't stop crying.

458

머릿속에 가득 담고 싶다.

I never want to forget it.

= I want to remember it forever.

459

혼자만의 생각에 갇혀 있어.

He is trapped in his thoughts.

・**trap** : (위험한 장소·궁지에) 가두다

= He thinks too much.

460

그 정도는 껌이지.

It's a piece of cake.

= It's super easy.

461

맛이 갔구나.
What has he been smoking.

= He's gone crazy.

462

새빨간 거짓말이야.
It's a total lie.

= That's completely false.

463

너무 벅찬 일이야.
It's a heavy burden.

· **burden** : 짐
= It's overwhelming.
· **overwhelming** : 압도적인

464

근처에도 안 갔어.
Not even close.

= That's far from it.

465

모 아니면 도야.
All or nothing.

= Go big or go home.

466

대박이야!

That's awesome!

= That's amazing!
= That's wonderful!
= That's breathtaking!
  • breathtaking : 숨이 막히는

467

소금을 들이부었나 봐.

It's like sea water.

= You put too much salt.

468

내가 먹어 본 것 중에 제일 맛있어.

It's the best I've ever had.

= It's the best thing I have ever eaten.

469

아직 덜 익었어.

It's not ripe yet.

• ripe : 익은
= It's not ready yet.

470

애들은 정말 금방 커.

Kids grow fast.

• grow : 성장하다, (크기·수·강도·특질이) 커지다,
  늘어나다

평가/판단

471

도토리 키 재기야.

There's not much of a difference.

= They are basically the same.
- basically : 기본적으로

472

너한텐 쉬운 말이겠지.

It might be easy for you to say.

= It's probably easy for you to say.

473

가성비 괜찮아.

It's cost-efficient.

= It's cost-effective.

474

정말 눈 깜짝할 사이였어.

It happened in a split second.

- split : 갈라진, 분리된, 쪼개진

= It happened in a flash.
- flash : 섬광, (잠깐) 반짝임
= It happened in the blink of an eye.
- blink : 눈을 깜빡거림

475

그럴 줄 알았어.

I figured that.

= I knew that.

476

실망이야.

Bummer.

· bummer : 실망(스러운 일)

= That's too bad.

477

강심장이네.

You've got guts.

· guts : 내장, 배짱

= You're brave.
= You're fearless.

478

그럴 만한 가치가 있어.

It's worth it!

· worth : (형용사) ~의 가치가 있는 (되는)

479

큰 발전이야.

That's a big step.

= That's a big change.

480

피장파장이야.

We're the same.

= We're similar.

CHAPTER 24
고민

481

나 고민 있어.

I have a concern.

= I got a problem.
= I have an issue.
= I'm worried.

482

나랑 같은 고민이구나.

I have the same problem.

= I got the same issue.
= I got the same concern.
  • concern : 고민, 걱정

483

정말 고민이야.

That's a real problem.

= That's a serious issue.

484

네가 그걸 고민하는지 몰랐어.

**I didn't know you were
worried about it.**

= I didn't know it worried you.

485

진작 말을 하지.

You should've told me earlier.

= You shouldn't have kept that for yourself.

486

그동안 힘들었어.

I had a hard time.

= I had a tough time.

487

상담 센터에 전화해 볼까?

Should I call a therapist?

• **therapist** : 치료 전문가, 치료사

= Do you want me to contact a counselor?
  • **contact** : 연락하다
  • **counselor** : 상담원, 상담사

488

일 년 동안 고민했어.

I have worried about it for a year.

= I was concerned about that for a year.

489

고민 끝에 깨달았어.

I eventually realized it.

• **eventually** : 마침내, 결국
• **realize** : ~을/를 깨닫다

490

내 고민이 우스워?

Does my concern seem like nothing to you?

= You don't take my problems seriously?

CHAPTER 24
고민

491

너는 고민이 없을 것 같아.

**You don't seem to
have a problem.**

= You don't look like you have any concerns.

492

성적이 고민이야.

I'm worried about my grade.

- **grade** : 성적
  = I'm concerned about my school grades.

493

난 외모 콤플렉스가 있어.

**I'm insecure about
my appearance.**

- **insecure** : 자신이 없는, 불안정한
- **appearance** : 외모
  = I am not confident about my appearance.
  - **confident** : 자신감 있는

494

저런 사람도 고민이 있을까?

I wonder if he has problems.

= I'm curious to know if he has any concerns.

495

마음 놓고 털어놔.

Spit it out.

- **spit** : (입에 든 음식 등을) 뱉다
  = Just say it already.

496

말하니까 속이 후련하다.

I feel better after talking to you.

= Now that I told you, I feel much lighter.

497

그게 무슨 고민이니?

What kind of concern is that?

= Is that really a problem?

498

답은 하나야.

You only have one choice.

= There's only one solution.

499

답은 간단해.

Your answer is simple.

= The key to this issue is obvious.
 • obvious : (눈으로 보거나 이해하기에) 명백한

500

네 고민 말해 줘서 고마워.

**Thanks for sharing
your concerns.**

• share : ~을/를 나누어 주다
= Thank you for telling me what's on
  your mind.

CHAPTER 25
위로/격려

501

눈물 닦아.

Wipe your tears.

- wipe : ~을/를 닦다
- tears : 눈물

= Stop crying.

502

네 심정 이해해.

I understand your feeling.

= I totally get how you feel.

503

네 잘못이라는 게 아냐.

I am not blaming you.

= You didn't do anything wrong.
= I'm not saying it's your fault.

504

너무 자책하지 마.

Don't blame yourself too much.

= Don't feel too bad about this.

505

얻는 게 있으면 잃는 것도 있어!

You can't have your cake and eat it too!

= You win some, you lose some.

506

걱정하지 마.

Don't worry.

= It'll be all right.
= Everything will be OK.

507

차라리 잘된 일일지도 몰라.

**It will probably open
other doors for you.**

= It's possibly better that way.

508

울고 싶으면 울어.

If you want to cry, then cry.

· **If you want to + 동사원형**
　　　　　　: 네가 만약 ~하고 싶다면

509

이 또한 지나가리라.

Everything will be OK.

= It'll pass.
= It'll be fine.
= It'll be all right.
= You'll get over it.

510

기운 내.

Cheer up.

= Stay strong.

위로/격려

511

긍정적으로 생각해.

Think positively.

- positively : 긍정적으로
= Be more optimistic.
  - optimistic : 낙천적으로
= Be positive about it.

512

조금만 더 힘내!

You are almost there!

= You can almost see the light at the end of the tunnel.

513

나랑 같이 해 보자.

Let's do it together.

= Let's work on this together.
= I'll help you with this.

514

네 가능성을 믿어.

I believe in your potential.

- potential : 잠재력, 잠재성
= I believe in you.
= I have faith in you.

515

넌 최선을 다했어.

You did your best.

= You tried your best.
= You did everything you could.

516

밑져야 본전이야.

It's worth trying.

= You've got nothing to lose. Just try it.

517

시작이 반이라잖아.

Starting is half the battle.

- **half** : 절반
- **battle** : 전쟁, 전투
- **half the battle** : (일의 가장 중요하거나 힘든 단계인) 고비

518

잘될 거야.

Everything will be fine.

= It'll be OK.
= Everything will go well.

519

방법이 있을 거야.

There must be a way.

= There has to be a solution.

520

너는 그렇게 약하지 않아.

You are not that weak.

= You're not that fragile.
- **fragile** : 부서지기 쉬운

CHAPTER 26
위로/격려

521

너는 충분히 강해.

You are tough enough.

= You're strong enough.

522

이대로만 해.

Keep it up.

= Continue that way.
= Keep that pace.

523

나 좀 응원해 줘.

Encourage me.

= Give me some support.

524

오늘만 날이 아니잖아.

Today is not the only day.

· 명사1 + **be not the only** + 명사2
　　: '명사1'이 유일한 '명사2'는 아니다

525

넌 아직 어리잖아.

You're still young.

= You have your whole life in front of you.

526

무엇이든 할 수 있어.

You can do everything.

= There are no limits to what you can do.

527

넘어져도 다시 일어나면 돼.

**You've got to get up,
if you fall down.**

= You can get through this.
= If you fail, try try again.

528

널 위해 기도할게.

I'll pray for you.

• **pray** : 기도하다
= I'll keep you in my prayers.

529

네 뒤엔 항상 내가 있어.

I've got your back.

= I'm here for you.

530

당당하게 하고 와.

Do it confidently.

• **confidently** : 자신 있게, 당당하게
= Just be who you are and be proud of
  yourself.

위로/격려

531

아직 끝나지 않았어.
It's not over yet.

= It's not the end.

532

호~ 해 줄게.
I'll kiss it better.

• **kiss it better** : 아픈 부위에 호~ 해 주다

533

우리 행복하자.
Let's be happy together.

= We will live happily together.

534

아무도 신경 안 써.
Nobody cares.

= No one cares.

535

마음 편하게 가져.
Take it easy.

= Ease your mind.

536

그럴 수도 있지.

That could be.

= That might be.

537

괜찮아질 거야.

That'd be fine.

= It'll get better.
= It'll be OK.
= Everything will be fine.

538

함께 있어 줄게.

I'll keep you company.

• company : 동료, 회사
= I'll stay with you.
= I'll stay by your side.

539

다행이야.

Oh, that's good.

= Good to know.
= That's a relief.

540

진정해.

Relax/Calm down/Take it easy.

= Chill out.
= Pull oneself together.

CHAPTER 27
사과/후회/용서

541

시끄럽게 해서 미안해.

I am sorry for being noisy.

= Excuse me for being so loud.

542

약속 못 지켜서 미안해.

**I am sorry for breaking
my promise.**

= I'm sorry that I didn't keep our promise.

543

귀찮게 해서 미안해.

I am sorry for bugging you.

• bug : 괴롭히다, 도청 장치를 달다
  = I'm sorry to bother you.

544

방해가 되었다면 미안해.

I am sorry if I interrupted you.

• interrupt : (말·행동을) 방해하다, 중단시키다
  = Pardon me for disturbing you.

545

진심으로 사과할게.

I truly apologize.

• apologize : 사과하다
  = I am sincerely sorry.

546

다 내 탓이야.

It's all my fault.

= It's all because of me.
= I was wrong.

547

기분 나빠하지 마.

No offence.

• offence : 위법 행위, 범죄, 화나게 하는 행위
  = I didn't mean to offend you.

548

개인적인 감정은 없어.

Nothing personal.

• personal : 개인적인
  = It's nothing against you.

549

깊이 반성하는 중이야.

I am seriously regretting it.

• regret : ~을/를 후회하다
  = I wish I could take back what I did.

550

내 실수라는 걸 깨달았어.

I found out about my mistakes.

• find out about + 명사 : ~에 대해 알아내다

CHAPTER 27
사과/후회/용서

551

나도 후회하고 있어.

I am also regretting it.

= I really feel bad about it.

552

내가 왜 그랬을까?

Why did I do it?

= What pushed me to act that way?

553

내가 태어난 게 잘못이다.

I should never have been born.

= I don't deserve to exist.

554

시간을 돌릴 수 있다면.

If I could go back in time.

= If only I could turn back time.

555

그러지 말았어야 했는데.

I shouldn't have done this.

= I really regret doing this.

556

다시는 이런 일 없을 거야.

This won't happen again.

= I'll make sure it does not happen again.

557

난 왜 하는 일마다 이 모양일까?

Can't I do anything right?

= Why do I always mess up everything?

558

내가 책임질게.

I will be responsible.

= I will take responsibility.

559

이 실수를 만회할 수 있을까?

How can I make up for my mistake?

= How can I compensate for what I did?
· compensate for : ~을/를 보상하다, 보충하다

560

다시는 안 그럴게.

I won't do it again.

= It won't happen again.

CHAPTER 28
사과/후회/용서

561

한 번만 기회를 줘.

Give me another chance.

= Give me another opportunity.

562

이제 그만 용서해 줘.

Forgive me now.

= Pardon me now.

563

용서해 주면 안 돼?

Can't you forgive me?

= Can't you pardon me?

564

제발 용서해 줘.

Please forgive me.

= I beg you pardon.

565

무릎 꿇고 빌까?

Should I kneel?

• kneel : 무릎을 꿇다

= Should I get on my knees?

566

눈앞에서 사라져 줘.

Get away from me.

= I don't want to see you anymore.

567

사과는 받는 사람 마음이야.

It's their choice to accept the apology.

· accept the apololgy : 용서하다

568

그게 사과야?

Is that an apology?

· apology : 사과

569

사과하지 마.

Don't apologize.

= Don't make any excuses.

570

용서 못 해.

I can't forgive you.

= I can't let this go.

CHAPTER 28
사과/후회/용서

571

미안하다고 몇 번 말해?

**How many times
should I apologize?**

= How many times should I say sorry?

572

내가 그렇게 잘못했니?

What have I done that's so bad?

= What I did was that wrong?

573

얼마나 더 빌어야 돼?

How much more should I beg?

• **beg** : 빌다
= How longer should I beg for?

574

그러는 넌 잘못 없어?

**You don't have
any responsibilities?**

= I'm not the only one who's
responsible for this.

575

나 말고 그 애한테 사과해.

**Don't apologize to me,
apologize to him.**

= Don't say sorry to me, say that to him.

576

어떻게 용서해 달라고 할 수 있어?

**How dare you ask me
for forgiveness?**

= Do you really think you have the right
to ask me for forgiveness?

577

봐줄게.

I will forgive you.

= I'll let it go this time.

578

이번이 마지막이야.

This is your last chance.

= This is the only opportunity I will give
you.

579

너 그러지 않겠다고 약속해.

**Promise me
it won't happen again.**

= Assure me you won't do this again.
 • assure : ~에 대해 확신시키다, 장담하다

580

아직도 용서가 안 돼.

I still can't forgive you.

= I can't get it over yet.

131

581

내 잘못이 아냐.

It's not my fault.

= You can't put the blame on me.

582

사정이 있었어.

I have an excuse.

= I have a good reason.
= There's a story behind this.

583

고의가 아냐.

I didn't mean it.

= I didn't do it on purpose.

584

난 정말 몰랐어.

I did not know.

= I had no idea.
= I had no clue.
  ·clue : 실마리

585

모르는 일이야.

I have no idea about it.

= I don't know anything about it.

586

기억이 잘 안 나.

I can't remember.

= I can't think of it.

587

난 좋은 뜻이었어.

I had good intentions.

· intention : 의도
= I meant to do good.

588

난 웃자고 그런 거야.

I just said it for fun.

= I didn't mean it.
= I said it just for fun.

589

이럴 줄 알았겠니?

**How could I know
this would happen?**

= Do you think I knew this would happen?

590

날 탓하지 마.

Don't blame me.

= Don't but the blame on me.
= Don't tell me it's my fault.

CHAPTER 29
변명

591

미안하지만 어쩔 수 없어.

I am sorry but I had no choice.

= Excuse me but there was no other way.
= Pardon me but it was the only thing
  I could do.

592

그런 의도는 아니었을 거야.

She did not mean it.

= She didn't really want to do that.

593

난 시키는 대로 했을 뿐이야.

I did what I was asked.

= I only followed orders.
  • order : 명령, 지침

594

알았으면 안 그랬겠지.

**I wouldn't have done it,
If I had known.**

= If I had been aware of that, I wouldn't
  have made that mistake.

595

너만 힘든 거 아니야.

**You are not the only person
with difficulties.**

= Everyone has problems.

596

그런 말 많이 들어.

I get that a lot.

= I hear that often.

597

어쩔 수 없는 일이었어.

It was unavoidable.

· unavoidable : 피할 수 없는

= There was no other way.

598

차가 막혔어.

I was stuck in traffic.

= There was a traffic jam.

599

오다가 사고가 났어.

I had an accident on the way.

= I got into an accident on my way.

600

버스가 늦게 왔어.

The bus came late.

= The bus arrived later than expected.

CHAPTER 29
변명

601

엄마가 시켰어.
Mom told me to.

= Mom asked me to.

602

집에 일이 있었어.
Something happened at home.

= There was an issue at home.

603

오늘 제정신이 아니야.
I'm not myself today.

= I'm not myself : 난 제정신이 아니다
 · You're not yourself : 넌 제정신이 아니다

604

깜빡했어.
It slipped my mind.

· slip : (어떤 위치·손을 벗어나) 미끄러지다,
   빠져나가다
= I completely forgot.

605

큰일은 아니야.
It's not a big deal.

= No big deal.
= It's not a problem.
= It's nothing to worry about.

CHAPTER 30
욕구/각오

606

더 자고 싶어.

I want to sleep more.

= I wish I could get more sleep.

607

졸려 죽겠네.

I'm dying to sleep.

= I'm dead tired.
= I'm exhausted.

608

낮잠 자고 싶어.

I want to take a nap.

• **take a nap** : 낮잠 자다
= I want to nap.

609

잠이 안 와.

I can't sleep.

= I have insomnia.
  • insomnia : 불면증

610

너무 많이 잤나 봐.

I slept too much.

= I overslept.
  • oversleep : 늦잠 자다

CHAPTER 30
욕구/각오

611

식욕이 없다.

I have no appetite.

- appetite : 식욕
= I'm not hungry.

612

배에서 꼬르륵 소리 나.

My stomach is growling.

- growl : (개들이) 으르렁거리다,
  (천둥 등이) 울리다
= My stomach is making noises.
  - stomach : 위, 위장
  - make noises : 소리 나다

613

그걸 먹느니 굶을래.

I would rather starve.

- starve : 굶다
= I'd prefer not eating than having that.

614

배에 거지가 들었나 봐.

**I feel like I have
a bottomless stomach.**

= My stomach is a bottomless pit.
  - bottomless : 바닥이 안 보이는, 무한한

615

슬슬 배고픈데?

I am starting to feel hungry.

= I'm slowly getting hungry.

616

배고파 죽겠네.

I am starving.

= I could eat a horse now!

617

소화가 잘 안 돼.

I have a digestive problem.

• digestive : 소화가 되는
= I have indigestion.
 • indigestion : 소화 불량

618

나도 그거 갖고 싶어.

I want that too.

= I wish I could get that too.

619

이거 너 주고 싶어.

I want to give this to you.

= This is a gift for you.
= This is a present for you.

620

오늘부터 금주야.

I've quit drinking from today.

= Starting today, I've stopped drinking.

CHAPTER 30
욕구/각오

621

오늘부터 금연이야.

I've quit smoking from today.

= From now on, I'm done smoking.

622

내 유일한 낙이야.

It's my only form of entertainment.

= It's my only hobby.

623

만사가 귀찮아.

I don't want to do anything.

= I don't want to move.

624

아무것도 하기 싫어.

I don't want to do anything.

= I feel lazy.

625

훌쩍 떠나고 싶어.

I just want to run away/escape/ get out of here/leave.

· run away : ~에서 달아나다
· escape : 탈출하다
· get out of : ~에서 떠나다/나가다
· leave : (사람·장소에서) 떠나다/출발하다

626

어디로든 떠나고 싶어.

I want to be anywhere besides here.

• besides : (전치사) ~ 외에

627

두고 봐.

You won't get away with it.

= You're going to get in trouble for this.

628

이제 내가 다 할게.

I will do it myself.

= I'll do it all on my own.

629

노력할게.

I will make an effort.

= I'll try my best.
= I'll do what I can.
  • make an effort : 수고하다, 노력하다

630

최선을 다할게.

I will try my best.

= I'll give it my all.

CHAPTER 31
제안/부탁

631

배달 음식 시켜 먹자.

Let's get delivery.

= Let's order food.
= Let's order in.

632

그냥 간단하게 때우자.

Let's grab something small.

= Let's get something little.

633

간단히 먹자.

Let's have a simple meal.

= Let's have a little something to eat.
= Let's have a snack.

634

나 한 입만 줘.

Give me a bite.
Let me taste.

• bite : 한 입(베어 문 조각), 소량의 음식, 요기
• Let + 사람 '목적격'/사물 '목적격' + 동사
         : ~을/를 ~하게 하다, 놔두다
ex) There are squirrels under the tree,
     let's get them!
     No, let them go.

635

점심 먹고 쉬었다 하자.

Let's take a lunch break.

= Let's take some time off for lunch.
= Let's break for lunch.

636

오늘 메뉴는 네가 골라.

You choose what you want.

= Pick whichever you want.

637

오늘은 너 먹고 싶은 거 먹자.

Let's eat what you want to eat.

= Let's have whatever you feel like eating.

638

머리 좀 식히자.

Let's take a break.

= Let's take five.

639

나갔다 올래?

Want to go out for a while?

= Want to get some fresh air?

640

스트레스 풀러 가자.

Let's go relieve some stress.

- **relieve** : 경감시키다, 안정시키다
- **relieve stress** : 스트레스를 풀다

641

오늘은 그만하자.

That's good for today.

= Let's call it a day.
= That's enough for today.
= Let's stop here for today.

642

여기까지만 하자.

Let's call it a day.

= Let's stop here.

643

쉬었다 가자.

Let's take a break.

= Let's take some time off.
= Let's rest for a bit.

644

가까우니까 걸어가자.

It's close so let's just walk.

= Let's just walk there since it's not far.

645

오늘은 일찍 들어가자.

Let's go home early.

= Let's leave sooner than usual today.

646

너도 와/너도 해!

Come with us!

= Accompany us.
· accompany : 동행하다

647

실력 발휘해 봐.

Show me your skills.

= Show me how good you are.
= Show us what you can do!

648

제대로 보여 줘.

Show me the right way.

= Show me how it's done.

649

나 이거 사줘.

Can you buy this for me?

= Could you get this for me?

650

자세히 말해 봐.

Please elaborate.

· elaborate : 더 자세히 설명하다
= Tell me the details.
= Please explain a little more.

CHAPTER 32
제안/부탁

651

용건만 말해.

Get to the point.

= Cut to the chase.
• chase : 추적, 추격

652

바쁘니까 나중에 얘기해.

Tell me later.

= I am busy now.
= I'm tied up so tell me later.

653

궁금하게 하지 말고 말해 줘.

Just tell me.

= Don't make me fret about it.
• fret about : ~에 대해 초조해하다, 안달하다

654

크게 얘기해 줄래?

Could you speak louder?

= Could you speak up?

655

할 말 있어.

I have something to tell you.

= There's something I need to tell you.

656

뭐 말해 줄게.

Let me tell you something.

= Now, listen to me.

657

말해 줄게.

I've gotta tell you.

= I'll talk to you about it.

658

끝으로 하나만 더 말할게.

One last thing.

• one last + 명사 : 마지막으로 한 번 더 ~
ex) one last look : 마지막으로 한 번 더 보기
　　　one last time : 마지막으로 한 번
　　　one last breath : 마지막 숨

659

그냥 넘어가.

Forget about it.

= Never mind.

660

예쁘게 찍어 줘.

Take a nice picture of me.

= Snap a nice picture of me.

661

나 옷 좀 빌려 줘.
Can I borrow your clothes?

= Could you lend me your clothes?

662

똑같이 반으로 나눠 줘.
Split it in half.

• split : (작은 부분들로) 나뉘다, 나누다
= Cut it in half.

663

반려동물을 아껴 주세요.
Take good care of your pet.

= Treat your pet well.
  • treat : 다루다

664

비위 좀 맞춰 봐.
Satisfy him.

= Make him happy.

665

재롱떨어 봐.
Impress me.

• impress : 인상 깊게 만들다
= Show me something cool.

666

양보해 줘.

Make way.
Would you please excuse me?

= Give me some room.

667

물러나.

Back off.

- ~ off : '떠나다, 물러가다, ~을/를 위해 제자리에서 이동하다, 벗어나다'의 뜻이 있음

668

계속 소식 전해 줘./올려 줘.

Keep me updated.

- updated : 업데이트된
- keep + 사람 '목적격' + 동사 pp
  : 계속 ~을/를 해 주다

669

조금만 기다려.

Hang in there.

= It's almost over.

670

어때?

What do you say?

= How is it?
= What do you think about it?

CHAPTER 32
제안/부탁

671

들어 봐.

Listen.

= Hear me out.

672

좀 놔둬.

Let it go.

= Leave me alone.

673

기대돼.

I can't wait.

= I'm looking forward to it.
= I'm excited for it.

674

이렇게 하자.

Here's the deal.

= Let's do it this way.

675

봐 봐.

Take a look at this.

= Check this out.
= Watch this.

의견

676

왜 이래?

C'mon!

= Are you serious?
= What are you doing?

677

있잖아.

You know.

· You know : 있잖아, 그러니까…
(다음 할 말을 생각할 때 쓰거나,
다음 할 말 앞에 운을 띄우기 위
해 씀)

678

내 말 뜻은~

I mean~

= What I mean is…
= What I'm trying to say is…

679

너 그거 알아?

You know what?

= Did you hear about that?

680

알아?

Guess what?

= You won't believe this.

CHAPTER 33
의견

있잖아.
Here's the thing.

= This is the point.

최소한/적어도
At least.

• **least** : (크기·양·정도 등이) 가장 적은(작은),
  최소의

그런데
By the way.

= Just so you know.

뭐든지
Whatever.

= Anything.
= No matter what.

아무튼
Anyway.

= Anyhow.
= In any case.

686

네 생각은 어때?

What do you think?

= How's that?

687

이렇게 하면 어때?

How about this?

= What about this?
= How about we do it this way?

688

그 의견에 동의해?

Do you agree with him?

• agree with ~ : ~에 동의하다
= Do you think the same as him?

689

둘 중 뭐가 나아?

Which one is better?

= Which one is the best?

690

네가 원하는 게 뭔데?

What do you want?

= What are you hoping for?
= What do you wish for?

691

할 거야, 말 거야?

So you want to do it or not?

= Are you in?
= Are you down?

692

왜 그렇게 생각해?

Why do you think that way?

= Why do you think like that?

693

가능성은?

What are the odds?

• **odds** : (어떤 일이 있을) 공산, 가능성
= What are the chances?

694

다르게 생각해 보자.

Let's try another route.

• **route** : 일 경로, 진행 방향
= Let's see it from another point of view.

695

내 입장에서 생각해 봐.

Put yourself in my shoes.

= Try to see it from my perspective.
= What would you do if you were me?

696

한번 볼까.

Let me see.

= Let me take a look.

697

요점은 ~

The point is ~

= The main idea is ~

698

내 생각엔 말이야.

I think.

= I believe.
= In my opinion.

699

내 경험상 ~

Based on my experience.

= From what I've seen.

710

내가 듣기로는

From what I have heard.

= I heard that ~

의견

701

내가 알기로는

From what I know.

• From what + 주어 + 동사 ~ : ~하는 바로는

702

나로서는 ~

For my part.

= Personally.

703

내 소견으로는

In my opinion

= I believe
= I think
= I suppose

704

나라면 ~

As for me.

= Personally.

705

우리가 아는 한

For all we know.

= As far as we know.

706

간단히 말하면

In a nutshell.

· nutshell : 아주 작은 그릇, 요약
= Simply.
= Briefly.

707

바꿔 말하면,

In other words.

= To say it another way.

708

화제를 바꿔서

Let's change the topic.

= Let's talk about something else.
= Let's change subjects.

709

말이 나와서 말인데.

Since we are talking about it.

= While we're on the subject.

710

정 그렇다면

If you insist.

= If that's what you really want.

CHAPTER 34
의견

711

다시 생각해.

Reconsider it.

- reconsider : 재고하다
= Think again.

712

싫으면 싫다고 해.

Tell me if you don't want it.

= If you don't like it, just say so.

713

생각해 보고 얘기해 줘.

**Let me know
after you think about it.**

= Sleep on it and give me your response.

714

생각할 시간을 줘.

Give me some time to consider.

= I need some time to think about it.
= Let me think about it for a while.

715

꼭 그렇다고 할 순 없어.

I can't really say.

= I'm not sure.
= I'm not positive about it.

CHAPTER 35
의견

716

다른 의견이 있어.

I have a different opinion.

= I have another idea.

717

별로 다를 거 없어.

It makes no difference.

= It's just the same.
= Nothing changed.

718

어떻게 대답해야 될지 모르겠어.

I don't know what to say.

= I'm not sure what I'm supposed to say.
  · be supposed to + 동사원형
      : ~하기로 되어 있다, ~할 의무가 있다

719

선택의 폭이 너무 넓어.

We have too many options.

= There are too many choices.

720

나 못 정하겠어.

I can't make up my mind.

= I can't decide.
= I can't choose.

721

애매해.

It's so vague.

- vague : 모호한
= It's unclear.
= It's ambiguous.
  - ambiguous : 애매모호한

722

잘 모르겠어.

I have no idea.

= I don't know.
= I have no clue.

723

난 상관없어.

I don't mind.

= It doesn't matter to me.
= Anything is fine with me.

724

네 말이 다 맞아.

You are right.

= That's correct.
= That's accurate.
= That's precisely true.
  - precisely : 명확히, 꼭

725

내 말이 그 말이야.

That's what I mean.

= That's what I'm trying to say.

726

내 말이 바로 그 말이야.

You're telling me.

= That's exactly what I mean.
= That's what I'm saying.

727

좋은 결정이야.

Good call.

= Nice one.

728

(의견이) 좋은데.

Fair enough.

= That makes sense.

729

솔직히 말해서

To be honest, Actually.

= Honestly.
= Sincerely.

730

추가적으로

In addition.

= Also.
= Additionally.
= Along with.
= As well as.

의견

731

게다가

Moreover.

= Furthermore.

732

참고로

For your information.

= Just so you know.
= FYI

733

예를 들어

For example.

= For instance.
= Such as.

734

이를테면

So to speak.

= As it were.

735

즉

In other words

= Namely.
= That is to say.

736

동감이야.

I agree.

= I'm with you.

737

나도 같은 생각이야.

I do agree.

= I think the same.
= I have the same opinion.

738

일부만 찬성해.

I agree in part.

= I sort of agree.
= I kind of agree.

739

그 의견에 찬성이야.

I agree with that opinion.

= That sounds right to me.

740

나도 마찬가지야.

Same here. Me too.

• **same** : (형용사) 똑같은, 동일한
= Likewise.

CHAPTER 36
찬성/허락/긍정

741

나도 마찬가지야.

That makes two of us.

= I'm in the same situation.
= We're in the same boat.

742

난 네 편이야.

I'm with you.

= I'm on your side.

743

같은 처지네.

We're in the same boat.

= I feel your pain.

744

바로 그거야.

There you go.

= That's exactly it!
= That's perfect!

745

좋은 생각이다.

That's a great idea.

= Good thought.
= Well thought of you.

746

바로 그거야.

That's it.

= Now, you got it.
= That's a bull's-eye.

747

좋은 생각이다!

That sounds perfect.

= What a wonderful idea!

748

그 제안 마음에 들어.

I like that suggestion.

= That's my kind of idea.

749

난 그 말을 믿어.

I believe what he said.

= I trust his words.

750

그거 재미있겠다.

That sounds interesting.

= It could be fun.

CHAPTER 37
찬성/허락/긍정

751

나쁘지 않은데?

Not bad.

= Fairly good.
= Good enough.
= Pretty good.

752

네가 원하는 대로 해.

Do whatever you want.

= Do as you please.
= As you wish.

753

이렇게 해도 돼.

Do it this way.

= Do it like this.

754

맘대로 해.

Do whatever you want.

= Do as you please.
= As you wish.

755

할 수 있는 데까지 해 봐.

Do what you can.

= Try your best.

756

옳아.

Right on.

= Exactly.
= Correct.

757

맞아.

That's right.

= That's correct.
= That's accurate.
= That's true.

758

거 봐.

Told you.

= There you are.
= I said so.

759

물론이지.

Of course.

= Certainly.
= No problem.

760

그런 것 같아.

I think so.

= I believe so.
= I suppose so.
= Probably.

CHAPTER 37
찬성/허락/긍정

761

내 말 진심이야.

I mean it.

= I'm serious.
= Mark my words.

762

내 말 사실이야.

It's true.

= I'm telling the truth.

763

확실해.

No doubt.

= I'm positive.
  · positive : 긍정적인, 확신하는
= I assure you.
  · assure : 장담하다, 확약하다

764

확실해.

I'm sure.

= I'm certain.
= I'm confident.
= I'm positive.

765

확실해.

For sure.

= Certainly.
= A hundred percent.

CHAPTER 38
반대/거절/부정

766

난 동의하지 않아.

I don't agree.

= I'm not okay with that.
= That's not OK with me.

767

난 동의하지 않아.

I disagree.

• disagree : ~에 동의하지 않다
= I don't think that way.

768

유감이지만 동의 못 해.

**Sorry but
I cannot agree with that.**

= Unfortunately, I think that's wrong.

769

난 반대야.

I think the opposite.

• opposite : 다른 편의, (정)반대의
= I'm against it.

770

그건 말도 안 돼.

No way.

= That's nonsense.

771

네가 틀린 것 같아.

I think you are wrong.

= I believe you're mistaken.

772

미안하지만 그건 아닌 것 같아.

Sorry but that's not gonna work.

= Sorry but I can't see that happen.

773

의미 없는 일이야.

It's not worth it.

= It's not worth the trouble.
= It's not worth the effort.

774

그거 별로야.

That's not so good.

= That's not great.
= That's just OK.
= It's so so.

775

좋은 생각 아니야.

That's not a good idea.

= I wouldn't do that.

776

그렇게 하지 마.

Don't do that.

= Stop doing that.

777

꼭 이렇게 해야 돼?

Do you have to do this?

= Do you really need to act that way?

778

오늘은 안 돼.

Not today.

= Today's not the best.
= Today won't work.

779

어려울 것 같아.

It's not gonna work.

• gonna : 'going to ~'의 줄임 표현
• work : 일하다, (기계·장치 등을) 작동시키다,
　　　　효과가 발생하다, 영향을 미치다

780

하지 말라면 하지 마!

If I say don't do it, don't do it!

= Do as I say!

781

내 눈에 흙이 들어갈 때까지
Over my dead body.

= Never.
= Don't even think about it.

782

더 이상은 안 돼.
Enough is enough.

= Stop now.

783

그만 됐어.
That's enough.

= Stop it.
= Cut it out.

784

그만.
That's it.

= That's enough.
= Give it a rest.

785

그만뒀으면 좋겠어.
I want you to quit that.

= I wish you would stop that.

786

안 돼.
You are not allowed.

= You can't do it.

787

집어치워.
Stop this!

= Quit it.
= Cut it out.

788

안 믿어.
I don't buy it.

= I don't believe it.
= I don't trust this.

789

그렇게 생각 안 해.
I don't think so.

= I don't think that's right.

790

맹세코 난 아니야.
I swear I didn't do it.

= I promise it's not me.
• promise : ~에 대해 맹세하다

CHAPTER 39
반대/거절/부정

791

전혀 기억 안 나.

I don't remember anything.

= I can't think of it.

792

하늘에 맹세코 거짓말 아니야.

**I swear to god
that I am not lying.**

= I promise i'm telling the truth.

793

거짓말하기 싫어.

I don't want to lie.

= I hate to be dishonest.
· dishonest : 부정직한

794

잘 안 들려.

I can't hear you.

· hear : (들려오는 소리를) 듣다

795

절대 아니야.

No way.

= Definitely not.
= Never.

CHAPTER 40
질문/의문

796

괜찮아?

Are you okay?

= Is everything all right?

797

뭐가 문제야?

What's the matter?

= What's the problem?

798

왜 그래?

What's wrong?

= What's going on?

799

어때?

How's it going?

= How is it?

800

무슨 말을 하는 거야?

What are you talking about?

= What are you saying?
= What are you trying to say?

질문/의문

801

이게 무슨 일이지?

What's happening?

- **happen** : (특히 계획하지 않은 일이) 발생하다, 벌어지다

802

이게 무슨 일이야?

What's going on?

= What's up?
= What happened?

803

뭐가 대수야?

What's the big deal?

= Why do you make such a great deal out of it?

804

무슨 얘기 하고 있었지?

Where were we?

= What were we saying?

805

그 밖에

What else?

= Besides that?
- **besides** : 게다가, 그 밖에

806

그래서 뭐?

So what?

= And?
= So?

807

뭐 때문에?

For what?

= What for?
= Why?
= For what reason?
= Because of what?
= For what purpose?

808

정말 그게 다야?

Is that all?

= Anything else?

809

쟤는 왜 저래?

What's the deal with him?

= What's his problem?
= What's wrong with him?

810

누구 맘대로?

With whose permission?

= Who said that was OK?

CHAPTER 41
질문/의문

811

무슨 말인지 알겠어?

Do you know what I'm saying?

= Do you understand what I'm saying?
= Do you get it?

812

무슨 말인지 알겠어?

Do you know what I mean?

= Do you understand what I'm trying to say?

813

그게 뭔 말이야?

What do you mean?

= What are you saying?

814

그거 누가 한 말이야?

Who said that?

• Who said that?
: 자신이 뱉은 말을 다른 사람이 한 것처럼 무마
시키려고 할 때 자주 쓰는 표현

815

뭘 쳐다봐?

What are you looking at?

= Do you have a problem?

816

내가 뭐라고 해야 돼?

What should I say?

• What should I + 동사 ~ ?
: 어떤 방식/방법으로 '동사'에 해당하는 행위를
  해야 하는지 조언을 구할 때 쓰는 표현

817

도대체 뭐지?

What is this all about?

= Why is this happening?
= What's the fuss about?
  • fuss : 법석, 야단을 떨다

818

왜 이렇게 우울해 보여?

Why the long face?

= What's wrong?
= What happened?

819

잘 잤어?

Did you sleep well?

= Did you have a good night?

820

이제 잘 들려?

Do you hear me now?

= Can you hear what I'm saying now?
= Can you hear clearly now?

821

비법이 뭐야?

What is your secret?

= How do you do this?

822

누구한테 물어볼까?

Who should I ask?

- Who should I + 동사 ~ ?
: 누구에게 '동사'에 해당하는 행위를 해야 하는
  지 조언을 구할 때 쓰는 표현

823

내기할래?

You wanna bet?

= Let's see who's right.

824

나 못 믿어?

Don't you believe me?

= You don't trust me?

825

내 얼굴에 뭐 묻었어?

Is there something on my face?

= Take a picture, it lasts longer.

826

내 말 알겠어?

You got it?

= Understand?
= Capiche?

827

알아들었어.

I got it.

= Understood.

828

너무 어려워.

It's too hard.

= It's really difficult.

829

뭐라는 거야.

What are you saying?

= What does that mean?

830

다시 말해 봐.

Say it again.

= Say it one more time.

이해

831

천천히 말해 줘.

Talk slowly.

= Speak slowly.
= Take your time.

832

이해되고 있어.

I'm totally getting it.

= I get it now.
= I understand now.
= It's clear now.

833

이제 이해되네.

I get the picture.

= I understand generally.
= I get the overall meaning.

834

아, 이제 알겠다.

I get it now.

= I understand now.
= It's clear now.

835

그렇게 말하면 내가 어떻게 알아.

I'm not following you.

= How can I get it if you explain it that way?

836

무슨 말인지 하나도 못 알아듣겠어.

**I don't know what
you are talking about.**

= I don't get it.
= It's not clear.

837

말을 해야 알지.

You gotta say something.

• gotta : 'got to'의 줄임 표현, '~해야만 한다'
라는 뜻

838

너라면 날 이해하겠니?

You'd understand if it were you.

= If you were me, would you get it?

839

네 말 이해 못 하겠어.

I don't follow.

= You're confusing me.
• confuse : ~을/를 혼란시키다

840

무슨 말인지 모르겠어.

You lost me.

= I'm not following.

841

못 알아듣겠어.
I can't follow you.

= I can't get it.
= I don't understand.

842

내 말 이해하고 있지?
Do you follow me?

= Do you get it?
= Do you understand?

843

확실히 이해했어?
Is everything crystal clear?

• **crystal** : 수정, 크리스털 유리
= Did you get everything?
= Do you understand perfectly?

844

확실히 이해했어?
Did you understand completely?

= Did you get everything?
= Did you understand it all?

845

확실히 이해했어?
Did you understand perfectly?

= Did you get it entirely?
  • **entirely** : 전적으로, 확실히

CHAPTER 43
농담

846

농담이지?

Are you kidding me?

= Is this a joke?
= Are you serious?

847

웃자고 한 소리야.

I was just joking around.

= I was just kidding.
= I'm just playing with you.

848

농담이었어.

It was a joke.

• joke : 우스갯소리, 농담

849

농담이었어.

I was joking.

= I was kidding.
= I wasn't being serious.
= I was playing with you.

850

농담처럼 안 들렸어.

It didn't sound like a joke.

= I didn't seem like you were kidding.

851

그런 농담 싫어.
I don't like that kind of joke.

= I don't enjoy that kind of humor.

852

네 농담 때문에 불쾌해.
Your joke makes me feel bad.

= I don't like your sense of humor.

853

진짜 웃긴 말이네.
That's so funny.

= That's hilarious.
- hilarious : 아주 우스운, 재미있는

854

그런 농담은 어디서 배워?
Where did you learn that joke?

= How did you learn that joke?

855

농담과 진담도 구분 못 해?
Can't you tell it's a joke?

= Isn't it obvious that I'm joking?
- obvious : 명백한

856

듣는 사람이 웃어야 농담이야.

Do you think you're funny?

• Do you think + 구문 ~ ? : ~라고 생각하나요?

857

넌 이게 웃겨?

Do you think that's funny?

= Is that funny to you?

858

넌 이게 웃겨?

You think it's funny?

• You think + 구문 ~ ?
: 상대방의 반응에 대한 냉소적인 대답

859

진짜야.

I mean it.

= Really.
= It's true!
= I'm serious.

860

나 진지해.

I'm serious.

= I'm not kidding.
= I'm not joking.

농담

861

농담 그만하자.

Stop joking.

= Be serious.
= Stop playing with me.

862

농담이라 믿을게.

I will take it as a joke.

= I'm gonna pretend it was not meant to be serious.

863

웃기니까 웃지.

I'm laughing cause it's funny.

- **laugh** : (소리 내어) 웃다
- **cause** : 'because'의 줄임 표현

864

농담이야, 진담이야?

Are you serious or are you joking?

= Is this a joke or···?

865

너만 웃고 있어.

You are the only one laughing.

= You're the only one who thinks it's funny.

866

재미없다고 했지?

I told you it's not funny.

= I told you I didn't find that funny.

867

하나도 안 웃겨.

It is not funny at all.

= That's not amusing.

868

넌 정말 유머 감각이 없어.

**You don't have
a sense of humor.**

= You are lack of a sense of humor.

869

너 말고 다 웃던데.

**Everybody was laughing
except you.**

= Everyone but you was having fun.

870

최고의 농담이네.

**That's the funniest thing
I've ever heard.**

= I've never heard something so funny.

비밀/소문

871

이거 진짜 비밀인데.

This is a secret.

= You must keep this to yourself.

872

비밀 지켜 줄 거지?

Are you gonna keep this secret?

• **keep one's secret** : ~의 비밀을 지키다
= Are you going to keep this to yourself?

873

네가 내 비밀 말했어?

Did you tell my secret?

= Did you tell anyone about my secret?

874

걔한테는 비밀 얘기를 하면 안 돼.

Don't tell him your secrets.

= Don't talk to him about your secrets.

875

난 입이 무거워.

My lips are sealed.

• **lips** : 입술
• **seal** : 봉하다
= I'm going to keep it to myself.
= I'm not gonna talk about it.

876

넌 입이 너무 가벼워.

You're bad with secrets.

= Bite your tongue.

877

넌 비밀이 많아 보여.

You seem to have a lot of secrets.

= You look like you are hiding a lot.
- hide : 숨기다

878

나만 알고 싶어.

I want to keep it to myself.

= I want to keep it a secret.

879

우리끼리 하는 말인데.

It's only between us.

= Don't talk about it to anyone else.
= It's between you and me.

880

무덤까지 갖고 가자.

Let's take it to our grave.

- grave : 무덤
= Don't ever talk about it to anyone.

CHAPTER 44
비밀/소문

881

너 그 소문 들었어?

Have you heard the rumor?

= Did you hear that rumor?

882

어디서 들었어?

Where did you hear about it?

= Where did you hear that?
= Who told you that?

883

누가 그런 소문을 내고 다녀?

Who's talking about it?

= Who made that up?

884

아니 땐 굴뚝에 연기 나겠니?

Where there's smoke, there's fire.

= It must be true.

885

무슨 소문인데?

What's the rumor?

= What rumor are you talking about?

886

그런 소문이 한두 개니?

There are tons of rumors like that.

• tons of : 꽤 많은
= That's something you hear everywhere.

887

소문에 휘둘리지 마.

Don't get involved.

• get involved : 연루된, 관계된
= Stay out of this.

888

소문의 힘은 대단해.

Rumors spread fast.

• rumor : 소문, 유언비어
• spread : (사람들 사이로) 퍼지다, 확산되다

889

연예인들은 소문에 시달려.

There is always gossip in Hollywood.

• gossip : 소문, 험담
= Hollywood is full of rumors.

890

어떻게 소문이 안 났지?

Why does nobody know yet?

= How is there no rumor about this?
= How can there be no story about this?

891

소문대로구나.

It's exactly how they say.

= It's just like they say.

892

소문과는 좀 다르네.

The rumor isn't exactly true.

= That sounds quite different from what I heard.

893

그 소문이 사실이래.

The rumor is true.

= That story is real.

894

웃긴 소문이 돌고 있어.

Funny rumors are flying around.

= I keep hearing stories.

895

넌 소문에 느리구나.

You are so behind on the gossip.

• be behind : 뒤쳐지다
• gossip : 소문, 험담

896

그렇게 들었어.

That's what I heard.

• **That's what** + 주어 + 동사 : 그것이 ~한 것이다

897

이상한 소문이 들려.

There are strange rumors.

= There are weird stories.

898

섬뜩한 소문을 들었어.

I heard some terrible news.

= I heard something terrible.
= Someone told me a horrible story.

899

여태 몰랐어?

You didn't know?

= You were not aware of that?

900

이건 해외 토픽감이야!

This should make headlines!

• **headlines** : (신문 제 1면 머리기사의) 표제
= This is big news.

가장 많이 쓰는

부사를 나태내는

영어 표현

시간에 관한 표현을 할 때

확신에 찬 표현을 할 때

정도에 관한 표현을 할 때

상태/상황에 대한 표현을 할 때

자신의 의견을 논리적으로 표현할 때

CHAPTER 46
시간에 관한 표현을 할 때

---

01 이틀에 한 번꼴로

Every other day — 과거부터 현재까지 이어져 오는 평상시 습관을 나타낼 때

I vacuum the living room every other day.
나는 이틀에 한 번꼴로 진공청소기로 거실을 청소해.

02 저번에

The other day — 과거의 특정한 날을 나타낼 때

I met my cousin at the concert the other day.
나는 저번에 콘서트장에서 내 사촌을 만났어.

---

03 언젠가

Someday — 미래의 어느 훗날을 나타낼 때

Would you like to travel around the world someday?
당신은 언젠가 세계 일주를 하고 싶나요?

04 언젠가

One day — 미래 어느 시기나 과거의 특정한 날을 나타낼 때

One day, I was alone in the house.
언젠가 나는 집에 혼자 있었다.

---

05 당장은

For now — 현재 막 처해 있는 상황을 의미할 때

For now, you should focus on studying.
너는 당장은 공부에 집중해야 해.

06 지금부터

From now on — '지금, 이 시점부터'라는 계속적인 시간을 보다 더 강조할 때

From now on, you will be assigned to the marketing team.
지금부터, 당신은 마케팅 팀에 배정될 것입니다.

07 잠시 동안

For a while — 기한을 짐작할 수 있는 비교적 짧은 시간을 의미할 때

I will be busy for a while today.
나 오늘 잠시 동안 바쁠 것 같아.

08 당분간

For the time being — 기한이 정해져 있지 않은 비교적 긴 시간을 의미할 때

It's better to keep it a secret for the time being.
당분간 그건 비밀에 부치는 게 좋을 것 같아.

CHAPTER 46
시간에 관한 표현을 할 때

---

09 흔히, 자주

Frequently — 특정한 시간을 정해 놓지 않았지만 '자주 무엇을 할 때'를 나타낼 때

We see each other **frequently**.
우리는 서로 자주 본다.

10 정기적으로

Regularly — 특정한 시간을 정해 놓고서 '규칙적으로 무엇을 할 때'를 나타낼 때

They enjoy eating out **regularly**.
그들은 정기적으로 외식을 한다.

---

11 지금, 현재

Currently — '현재, 당연한 이 시점'을 가리킬 때

There are **currently** only two positions open.
현재 두 자리만이 비어 있습니다.

12 요즘

These days — '현재와 그리 멀지 않은 최근의 과거 시점'까지 포함하여 가리킬 때

The young generation **these days** tend to travel a lot.
요즘 청년 세대들은 여행을 많이 하는 추세이다.

---

⑬ 최근에, 요즘 들어

Recently — 과거의 단발적인 사건 및 현재까지 지속되는 사건을 가리킬 때

Recently, I've been getting home late from work.
요즘 들어, 나는 퇴근을 늦게 해 오고 있다.

⑭ 최근에

Lately — 현재까지 지속되는 사건만을 가리킬 때 (과거 단순 시제와 쓰이지 않음)

He has been very sensitive lately.
최근에 그는 굉장히 예민한 상태이다.

⑮ 자주

Often — '보다 다발적으로 무엇인가를 함'을 의미할 때

How often do you shampoo your hair?
당신은 머리를 얼마나 자주 감나요?

⑯ 가끔

Occasionally — '어떤 일이 일어나는 특정한 때에 맞춰 무엇인가를 함'을 의미할 때 ('sometimes'와 유사어)

My father cooks occasionally.
아버지는 요리를 가끔 하신다.

CHAPTER 46
시간에 관한 표현을 할 때

17 곧

Shortly — '어떤 일이 일어난 바로 그때'를 의미할 때

I will be home shortly.
나 곧 집에 도착해.

18 잠깐

Briefly — '어떤 일이 짧은 시간 동안 일어나거나 지속될 때'를 의미할 때

Could I talk to you briefly?
잠깐 이야기 나눌 수 있을까요?

19 즉시

Immediately — '지금, 당장'을 의미할 때

Come here immediately!
즉시 여기로 와!

20 머지않아

Soon — 지금 이 시점으로부터 멀지 않은 가까운 시점을 의미할 때

It soon became clear that the match was not interesting.
머지않아 경기가 흥미롭지 않다는 것이 분명해졌다.

21 빨리

Quickly — 얼마나 빠른 속도 내에 할 수 있는지를 나타내는 시간적 표현일 때

You need to finish your homework as **quickly** as possible.
너는 가능한 한 빨리 숙제를 마쳐야 할 거야.

22 갑자기

Suddenly — 순간적으로 갑작스럽게 일어난 상황을 나타내는 시간적 표현일 때

Somebody **suddenly** popped up in front of me.
누군가가 갑자기 내 앞에 불쑥 나타났다.

23 곧장

Directly — 물리적으로 즉시 실현이 가능한 상황·경우를 나타낼 때

You must call me **directly** after arriving.
너는 도착 후에 곧장 나에게 전화해야 해.

24 지체 없이

Promptly — 일반적으로 즉시, 신속하고 빠르게 처리하는 행위를 가리킬 때

The mission should be done **promptly**.
그 임무는 지체 없이 실행되어야 합니다.

CHAPTER 46
시간에 관한 표현을 할 때

25 이전에

Before — 과거의 모든 시점을 포함할 때

I never imagined that I would learn how to scuba dive, before.
나는 이전에 내가 스쿠버 다이빙을 배울 것이라고는 상상하지 못했다.

26 (과거) 언젠가

Once — 과거의 특정한 시점을 가리킬 때

I watched that film once and it turned out to be awesome.
언젠가 나는 그 영화를 본 적이 있었는데 아주 기가 막혔다.

27 첫 번째로, 우선

Firstly — '일련의 일어날 상황들의 가장 첫 단계'를 의미할 때

Firstly, you need to sign here.
우선, 당신은 이곳에 서명해야 합니다.

28 처음에

Initially — '일이나 상황의 시작점'을 의미할 때

Initially, he thought I didn't speak French.
처음에, 그는 내가 프랑스어를 못 하는 줄 알았다.

29 이른, 일찍

Early — '특정한 사건의 발생으로 인해 평상시보다 더 빠름'을 의미할 때

We went there too early!
우리 거기 너무 일찍 갔었어!

30 벌써

Already — 생각했었던 시기보다 앞서 발생한 상황을 표현할 때 쓰임

It's already winter!
벌써 겨울이야!

31 서서히

Gradually — '긴 시간 동안 조금씩 변하거나 이동해 감'을 의미할 때

The weather is gradually getting colder there days.
요즘엔 날씨가 서서히 추워지고 있어.

32 계속

Constantly — '긴 시간 동안 꾸준히 지속됨'을 의미할 때

My mother is constantly on my case.
우리 엄마는 내 일에 계속 참견 중이시다.

CHAPTER 47
확신에 찬 표현을 할 때

01 사실은

Actually — 어떤 상황에 대한 반전의 의미를 강조할 때

Actually I am not that rich.
사실은 나 그렇게 부자는 아니야.

02 진짜로

Really — 전달하고자 하는 바를 보다 더 강조할 때

You must be **really** happy!
너는 진짜로 행복하겠구나!

03 확실히/명백히

Obviously — 듣는 사람이 전달받는 상황을 이미 알고 있다고 생각할 때 강조하기 위하여

That girl is **obviously** into you.
저 여자애는 확실히 너한테 반했어.

04 또렷하게

Clearly — '명백한 결과나 사실' 혹은 '명확하고 분명한 인지'를 묘사할 때

Did you understand that **clearly**?
너는 저걸 또렷하게 이해했니?

05 틀림없이, 바로

Exactly — '자신이 말하고 있는 바와 명확히 일치하는 것'을 의미할 때

That's exactly what I am talking about!
바로 그게 내가 말하고 있는 거야!

06 바로/꼭/정확히

Precisely — 정확히 어떤 정보와 똑같을 때

The play begins at precisely 8 o'clock.
공연은 8시 정각에 시작한다.

07 분명히

Certainly — 자신이 강력히 믿거나 무엇이 사실임을 강조할 때

What you wrote here is certainly wrong.
네가 여기에 썼던 내용은 분명히 틀렸어.

08 반드시

For sure — 자신이 생각하고 있는 것에 대해 확신을 부여할 때

I will call you tonight for sure.
난 오늘 밤에 반드시 너를 부를 거야.

확신에 찬 표현을 할 때

09 절대로, 틀림없이

Absolutely — 매우 강한 동의나 결심을 표현할 때

You **absolutely** need to bring your lunch.
너는 반드시 네 점심을 가지고 와야 해.

10 절대로

Definitely — 자신이 전하고자 하는 의도나 의견을 강력히 강조하면서 표현할 때

I will **definitely** never climb that mountain again.
나는 절대로 저 산을 다시 올라가지 않겠어.

11 절대 아니다

Absolutely not — 매우 강한 부정이나 반대하는 경우를 표현할 때

Am I bothering you? **Absolutely not!**
내가 너를 귀찮게 하니? 절대 아니야!

12 결코 아니다

Definitely not — 자신이 하지 않으려는 바에 대해 강력히 표현할 때

He will **definitely not** go back to his country.
그는 결단코 그의 고국으로 돌아가지 않을 것이다.

13 매우

Highly — 표현하고자 하는 것의 정도가 최대인 경우

I highly recommend visiting that museum.
나는 그 박물관을 방문하기를 매우 추천한다.

14 단호히

Firmly — 어떠한 사안이나 상황에 대해 매우 견고한 의견임을 나타내는 경우

I always defend my opinions firmly.
나는 항상 내 의견을 단호히 피력한다.

CHAPTER 48
정도에 관한 표현을 할 때

01 심각하게

Seriously — 자신이 말하고자 하는 바가 어떠한 농담도 없이 그 자체일 때

He seriously hurt himself.
그는 자기 자신을 심각하게 다그쳐.

02 심하게

Heavily — 어떠한 현상·감정의 정도가 심하거나 심각할 때

You're coughing heavily today!
너 오늘 기침을 심하게 하는구나!

03 전적으로

Totally — 뒤에 나오는 어구를 강조하기 위해

We are totally lost now.
우리는 지금 전적으로 길을 잃었다.

04 몹시

Terribly — 주로 문장 전체를 강조하며 정도가 굉장히 심할 때

I terribly miss you.
나는 네가 몹시 보고 싶어.

05 모두

Fully — 정도나 가능성의 최대 지점을 의미하며 '모두'라는 의미로 사용할 때

Did you **fully** understand the essay?
너는 글을 모두 이해했니?

06 철저히/완벽히

Thoroughly — 자신이 하는 행동이나 생각이 빈틈없이 '완전함'의 의미로 사용할 때

She **thoroughly** enjoyed her experience.
그녀는 그녀의 경험을 완벽히 즐겼다.

07 완전히

Completely — 뒤에 나오는 어구를 강조하기 위해

I am not **completely** awake yet.
나 아직 완전히 깨진 않았어.

08 극히

Extremely — 어떠한 특성이 최대의 정도라는 것을 나타내기 위해

This task is **extremely** difficult.
이 일은 극도로 어렵다.

CHAPTER 48
정도에 관한 표현을 할 때

09 꽤

Fairly — 정도가 완전하지는 않지만 상당함을 의미할 때

That movie was **fairly** interesting.
그 영화는 꽤 흥미로웠어.

10 꽤/상당히

Reasonably — 어떤 상황과 비교해서 상당함을 의미할 때

The quality of the food was **reasonably** good.
음식의 질은 상당히 좋았어.

11 크게

Significantly — '영향을 미치거나 두드러질 정도로 정도가 큼'을 의미할 때

My salary increased **significantly**.
내 월급은 크게 상승하였다.

12 상당히

Substantially — '양의 정도가 상당히 큼'을 의미할 때

The average rent in Seoul has **substantially** increased.
서울의 평균 집세가 상당히 증가하였다.

13 많이

A lot — 말하고자 하는 것의 양이 많을 때

I had a lot of chores to do last weekend.
나 저번 주에 해야 할 집안일들이 너무 많았어.

14 대부분

Most — 사물이나 사람의 대다수를 의미할 때

Most people you meet in your life could give you some lessons to learn.
당신이 인생에서 만나는 대부분의 사람들은 당신에게 배울 만한 교훈을 준다.

15 대강

Roughly — 말하고자 하는 정보를 대략적으로 가늠했을 때

It takes roughly two hours to get to the airport from here.
이곳에서 공항까지 가는 데 대략 2시간가량 소요된다.

16 그냥/그저

Simply — 어떤 일이 얼마나 쉽거나 간단한지를 강조할 때

You can't leave simply because you are tired.
네가 피곤하다고 그냥 떠날 수는 없어.

정도에 관한 표현을 할 때

14 조금
Slightly — 어떤 현상이나 상황의 정도가 크지 않고 미약함을 나타낼 때

I feel slightly dizzy.
나는 조금 어지럽다.

18 약간
A bit — 양, 정도의 조그마함을 나타낼 때

Would you please turn the volume down a bit?
음량을 약간 줄여 주시겠어요?

19 깊이
Deeply — 믿음, 관습 등과 같이 정신적인 것의 정도가 깊음을 나타낼 때

I am deeply sorry for your loss.
당신의 상실감에 깊이 조의를 표합니다.

20 완전히
Completely — 눈에 보이는 것의 정도가 클 때 역시 나타냄

I think I completely fell in love with her.
나는 그녀와 완전히 사랑에 빠진 것 같아.

CHAPTER 49
상태/상황에 대한 표현을 할 때

01 전형적으로

Typically — 일반적으로 널리 인정되는 것을 나타낼 때

Typically, people eat turkey on Thanksgiving day.
전형적으로, 사람들은 추수감사절 날 칠면조를 먹는다.

02 전통적으로

Traditionally — 역사적으로, 관습적으로 통용되어 온 것을 나타낼 때

The marriage in Korea has traditionally been regarded as a family event.
한국에서의 결혼은 전통적으로 가족 행사로 여겨져 왔다.

03 대부분

Mostly — 어떠한 사물이나 사안의 일반적인 사실을 나타낼 때

What fabric is this shirt mostly made of?
이 셔츠는 대부분 어떤 천으로 만들어졌나요?

04 주로

Mainly — 어떠한 사물이나 사안의 주된 이유나 현상을 나타낼 때

Are your friends mainly from Canada?
너의 친구들은 주로 캐나다 출신이니?

CHAPTER 49
상태/상황에 대한 표현을 할 때

05 거의

Approximately — 뒤에 숫자가 위치해, 수리적으로 얼마나 근접했는지를 나타낼 때

Shipping takes approximately three days.
선적은 대략 사흘 정도가 소요됩니다.

06 거의

Almost — 어떠한 상황이나 경우가 완전히는 아니지만 최대로 실현됐음을 나타낼 때

She almost got into trouble this morning.
그녀는 오늘 아침 거의 곤경에 빠졌었다.

07 거의

Nearly — 어떠한 상황이나 경우가 완전히는 아니지만 최대로 실현됐음을 나타낼 때

John nearly missed his flight to Korea.
John은 한국으로 가는 비행기 편을 거의 놓칠 뻔했다.

08 드물게

Rarely — 무엇이 거의 나타나거나 일어나지 않음을 나타낼 때

My mother rarely wears black clothes.
우리 엄마는 검은색 옷을 드물게 입는다.

09 일반적으로

Generally — 상황이나 행동, 생각에서 주로 발생하거나 겪는 일을 나타낼 때

What do you **generally** do after dinner?
너는 일반적으로 저녁 식사 후에 무엇을 하니?

10 대개

Commonly — 상황이나 행동, 생각에서 주로 발생하거나 겪는 일을 나타낼 때

This computer is **commonly** used among students.
이 컴퓨터는 대개 학생들이 사용합니다.

11 보통/대개

Usually — 특정한 상황에서 자주 발생하는 것을 나타낼 때

My sister **usually** sleeps in on weekends.
우리 언니는 보통 주말 동안 늦잠을 잔다.

12 보통

Normally — 주로 일어나는 상황이나 주로 하는 것을 나타낼 때

I **normally** don't like broccoli, but this is tasty!
나는 보통 때는 브로콜리를 좋아하지 않지만 이건 맛있다!

CHAPTER 49
상태/상황에 대한 표현을 할 때

13 특히

Particularly — 말하고자 하는 바가 특별히 한 가지 상황이나 경우에 적용됨을 나타낼 때

Pay attention to the rules, **particularly** number five.
규칙을 준수하되, 특히 5번 사항은 더 유의하시길 바랍니다.

14 특히

Especially — 말하고자 하는 바가 특별히 한 가지 상황이나 경우에 적용됨을 나타낼 때

I like everything on their menu, **especially** the salmon.
나는 그 식당의 메뉴를 다 좋아하지만, 그중에서도 특히 연어가 좋다.

15 전적으로

Entirely — '부분적으로 해당되는 것이 아닌, 전체'를 나타낼 때

My class is made up **entirely** of women.
우리 교실은 전적으로 여자들로 구성되어 있다.

16 기본적으로

Basically — 자신의 의견이나 해당 상황에서 중요한 바를 나타낼 때

My grandfather **basically** goes to church every Sunday.
우리 할아버지는 기본적으로 매주 일요일마다 교회에 가신다.

17 원래

Originally — 추후에 일어난 상황과 반대되는 상황을 나타낼 때

Originally, I was not supposed to move here.
원래 나는 여기로 이사 올 예정이 없었어요.

18 본래

Essentially — 가장 중요하고 가장 기초가 되는 특징, 자질을 나타낼 때

Essentially, you just need to follow me.
본래 당신은 그저 나만 따라오면 되는 거예요.

19 새로

Newly — 특정한 행동이 굉장히 최신이거나 특정 사안이 가장 최근에 시작되었음을 나타낼 때

We are newly married.
우리 신혼이에요. / 우리 이제 막 결혼했어요.

20 순전히

Purely — 말하고자 하는 바가 가장 중요하고 유일한 특징임을 나타낼 때

I am asking this purely out of curiosity.
난 이걸 순전히 호기심에 물어보는 거야.

CHAPTER 49
상태/상황에 대한 표현을 할 때

21 똑같이

Equally — 양, 공간 등 모든 요소에서 균등함을 나타낼 때

We must love everyone **equally**.
우리는 모두를 똑같이 사랑해야 한다.

22 비슷하게

Similarly — 어떤 것이 다른 것과 유사함을 나타낼 때

These twins are always **similarly** dressed.
이 쌍둥이들은 항상 비슷하게 옷을 입는다.

23 기분 좋게, 다정하게

Nicely — 상황이나 일이 만족스럽고 자신이 원하는 방향으로 이루어짐을 나타낼 때

My boyfriend's mother treats me **nicely**.
내 남자 친구의 어머니는 나를 기분 좋게 대해 주신다.

24 친절하게

Kindly — 사려 깊고 도움이 되는 방향으로 행동함을 나타낼 때

The couple welcomed us **kindly**.
부부는 우리를 친절하게 맞이해 주었다.

25 걷잡을 수 없이, 거칠게

Wildly — 무엇을 격렬하고 극심하게 함을 나타낼 때

Soccer fans always cheer wildly.
축구 팬들은 항상 거칠게 응원한다.

26 필사적으로, 간절히

Desperately — 극도로 절박한 상황을 나타낼 때

I desperately need some money.
나 간절히 돈이 좀 필요해.

CHAPTER 50
자신의 의견을 논리적으로 표현할 때

---

01 겉보기에/표면상으로

Apparently — 말하고자 하는 정보가 완전히 맞지는 않지만 어느 정도 객관적임을 나타낼 때

Apparently, many things are complicated in this modern society.
현대 사회에서는 많은 것들이 복잡합니다.

02 당연히

Naturally — 어떠한 상황에서 무언가가 매우 명백하고 놀랍지 않음을 나타낼 때

Naturally, it makes me angry when you talk back to me.
네가 내 말을 받아치는데 당연히 내가 열이 받지.

---

03 개인적으로

Personally — 자신 개인의 의견을 피력함을 나타낼 때

Personally, I prefer spending time outside to staying at home.
나는 개인적으로 집에 있는 것보다 밖에서 시간 보내는 것을 선호한다.

04 개별적으로

Individually — 한데 묶여 나타나거나 시행되는 것이 아니라 각각 이루어짐을 나타낼 때

You have to meet your adviser individually.
교수님은 개별적으로 만나야 합니다.

---

05 일부

Partially — 상황이나 사안의 모든 부분에서 어느 정도를 나타낼 때

It's also partially your fault.
일부 네 과오도 있어.

06 부분적으로

Partly — 특히 무엇이 발생한 이유의 부분적인 원인을 나타낼 때

I enjoyed my trip in Spain, partly due to the nice weather.
나는 스페인에서 즐겁게 여행했는데, 부분적으로는 좋은 날씨 때문이었다.

07 솔직히

Honestly — 자신이나 다른 사람의 진실한 믿음이나 감정을 나타낼 때

Honestly, I think you should discuss it with him.
솔직히, 저는 당신이 그와 의논해 봐야 한다고 생각해요.

08 진실로, 진심으로

Truly — 어떠한 상황이나 사안이 최대한 가능함을 나타낼 때

The result of the election was truly unpredictable.
선거의 결과는 진실로 예상 불가능했다.

CHAPTER 50
자신의 의견을 논리적으로 표현할 때

09 기꺼이

Gladly — 어떠한 제안이나 요청을 기쁘게 받아들임을 나타낼 때

I would **gladly** help you if I had time.
내가 시간이 있다면 기꺼이 당신을 도울 것입니다.

10 바라건대

Hopefully — 바라는 바가 뜻대로 이뤄지길 소망함을 나타낼 때

Hopefully, I will attend the meeting on Thursday.
바라건대, 나는 목요일에 있을 회의에 참석하면 좋겠다.

11 유감이지만

Unfortunately — 슬픔과 실망, 후회를 나타낼 때

I **unfortunately** can't have Tuesday off.
유감이지만 난 화요일에 빠질 수 없어.

12 애석하게도

Sadly — 슬픔과 안타까움을 나타낼 때

Sadly, they had to go their separate ways in the end.
애석하게도 그들은 마지막에 각자의 길을 가야만 했다.

13 결국

Eventually — 많은 날과 문제를 겪고 난 이후의 결과를 나타낼 때

Eventually, you should think about asking for help.
당신은 결국 도움을 요청하는 것에 대해 생각해 봐야 한다.

14 마침내

Finally — 자신이 예상했던 것보다 긴 시간이 흐르고 난 뒤를 나타낼 때

I am finally done with my thesis.
마침내 나는 논문 작성을 마쳤다.

15 그 결과

Consequently — 어떠한 행위가 지속되어 나타낸 결과를 나타낼 때

Consequently, we don't have to discuss it.
그 결과, 우리는 그것에 대해 토론할 필요가 없다.

16 마찬가지로

Likewise — 두 가지의 방법, 상황, 사안 등이 유사함을 나타낼 때

Likewise, we are looking forward to it.
여러분과 마찬가지로, 우리도 그것을 기대하고 있어요.

CHAPTER 50
자신의 의견을 논리적으로 표현할 때

17 어쩌면

Probably — 확실치 않거나 어느 정도 예측되는 의미를 나타내는 표현일 때

I can **probably** make it on Saturday morning.
난 어쩌면 토요일 오전에 그걸 완성할 수 있다.

18 어쩌면 ~할 수도

Possibly — 미래에 일어날 수도 있는 가능성에 대한 표현일 때

My family said they would **possibly** visit me next month.
우리 가족은 어쩌면 다음 주쯤에 나를 보러 올 수도 있다고 얘기했다.

19 유일한, 오직

Only — 오직 하나라는 의미에 초점을 둔 표현일 때

She tends to think **only** about herself.
그녀는 그녀 자신만 생각하는 경향이 있다.

20 그저

Just — 말하고자 하는 의미 자체만을 강조하는 표현일 때

This suit is **just** my size.
이 정장은 딱 내 사이즈다.

21 제대로

Properly — 상황이나 처지에 알맞게 한다는 의미일 때

Why don't you ever do anything **properly**?
너는 왜 아무것도 제대로 하는 게 없니?

22 상당히, 꽤

Fairly — 주로 상황의 정도를 강조할 때

You will definitely think that the place is **fairly** amazing.
넌 분명히 그곳이 상당히 놀랍다고 생각하게 될 거야.

23 불가피하게

Inevitably — 피할 수 없이 맞닥뜨려야 한다는 의미로 필수적인 상황을 나타내는 표현일 때

You just **inevitably** didn't get a chance this time.
넌 이번에 그저 불가피하게 기회를 얻지 못했을 뿐이야.

24 어쩔 수 없이, 반드시

Necessarily — 반드시 꼭 있어야 한다는 의미를 강조할 때

All boys don't **necessarily** like cars and robots.
모든 남자 아이들이 꼭 자동차와 로봇을 좋아하는 것은 아니다.

CHAPTER 50
자신의 의견을 논리적으로 표현할 때

25 정신적으로

Mentally ─ 주로 '정신적으로'라는 의미를 표현할 때

His job is **mentally** challenging.
그의 직업은 정신적으로 쉽지 않은 일이다.

26 신체적으로

Physically ─ 주로 '신체적, 육체적으로'라는 의미를 표현할 때

My taekwondo lesson was **physically** exhausting.
나의 태권도 수업은 신체적으로 진을 빼 놓는다.

27 비교적

Relatively ─ 특정한 두 대상을 비교해서 표현할 때

Winter is **relatively** warmer in Jeju than in Seoul.
제주도의 겨울은 비교적 서울보다 따뜻하다.

28 비교적, 상당히

Comparatively ─ 특정한 두 대상을 비교해서 하나가 더 월등하다는 의미를 표현할 때

This book is **comparatively** cheap.
이 책은 상당히 싸다.

29 일부러

Deliberately — 신중히 생각을 하고 나서 어떤 의도성을 띄는 의미일 때

I am certain that he avoided me deliberately.
나는 그가 나를 일부러 피하고 있음을 확신했다.

30 고의로

Intentionally — 무엇을 꾀하기 위해서 계획적으로 상황을 전개하는 의미일 때

He used that word intentionally.
그는 고의로 그 단어를 사용했다.

31 쉽게

Easily — 상황이나 행동에 있어 어려움이 없다는 의미일 때

He can easily run ten kilometers without getting tired.
그는 10킬로미터를 지친 기색 없이 쉽게 완주할 수 있다.

32 유창하게

Fluently — 한 분야에 대해 전문가 수준으로 행동함을 나타낼 때

Can you really speak five languages fluently?
당신은 정말 5개 국어를 유창하게 하실 수 있나요?

33 따로따로

Separately — 서로 분리하고 떨어뜨려 보는 개별적 관점의 의미일 때

Could we please pay separately?
저희 따로따로 계산할 수 있을까요?

34 각각

Each — 어떤 한 무리 안에서 서로 떨어뜨려 보는 상대적 관점의 의미일 때

Each book will be displayed on the shelves by next week.
다음 주까지 각각의 책들이 진열대 위에 전시될 예정입니다.

35 공식적으로

Officially — 일반적으로 '대내외적으로 밝혀진 상태'를 의미할 때

They officially graduated from university.
그들은 공식적으로 대학교를 졸업하였다.

36 정식으로

Formally — 어떤 정해진 절차나 규정에 의해 밝혀진 상태를 의미할 때

The report has formally been accepted by the government.
정부는 정식으로 보고서를 받아들였다.

37 효과적으로

Effectively — 적정한 비용이나 노력에 맞는 알맞은 결과를 얻어냄을 의미할 때

You should use electricity more effectively.
당신은 전기를 보다 효과적으로 사용해야 한다.

38 능률적으로

Efficiently — 적은 비용이나 노력을 통해 극대화의 결과를 얻어냄을 의미할 때

He did the job quite efficiently.
그는 그 일을 꽤 능률적으로 해냈다.

39 충실히

Faithfully — 어떤 특정 대상에 대한 변함없는 마음을 의미할 때

I promise to love you faithfully until the end of time.
나는 영원히 당신을 충실히 사랑할 것을 맹세합니다.

40 진심으로

Sincerely — 어떤 상황이나 대상에 대해 진심을 표현할 때

Sincerely yours.
당신의 진실한 사람으로부터.

Special
thanks to

혼자 외로이 서 있을 때 조용히 옆에 와서
같이 머물러 준 고마운 분들이 계십니다.

늘 푸근한 서사모 조정환 매니져님,
늘 수고해 주시는 이남식 부매니져님,
언제나 기도해 주시는 홍승연 누님,
맏언니 같은 정미경 누님,
쓴소리 맏형 유정수 님,
가장 사랑받는 조소영 감독님,
늘 그림자같이 곁에서 애써 주시는
박현우 님, 윤경아 님, 한경혜 님, 박순덕 님, 이윤미 님,
박선주 님, 이연아 님, 이재영 님, 박주희 님, 김윤수 님,
장유정 님, 홍예나 님, 권오성 님, 고대경 님 그리고
늘 기다려 주시는 서일환 우리 아버지, 사랑하는 가족들,
어려운 환경에서 꿋꿋이 애써 준 토마토출판사 동료들
그 외에도 많은 스쳐가는 얼굴들, 정말 감사합니다.